Joseph

PISCHNA

SIXTY PROGRESSIVE ETUDES

FOR PIANO

K 03770

Preparatory Exercises to Nº 1ª

Practise in all keys.

Lento

J. Pischna.

Lento.

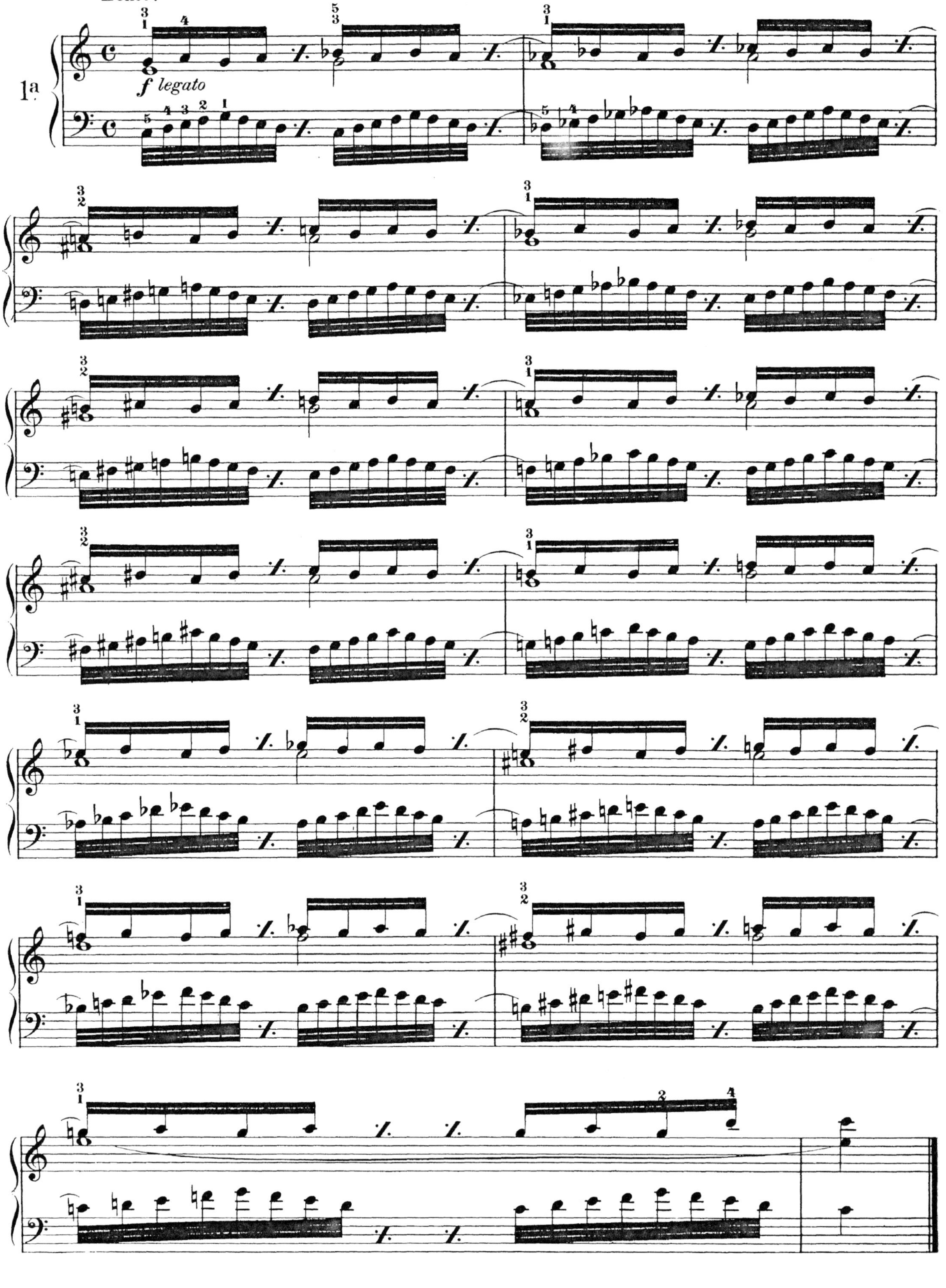

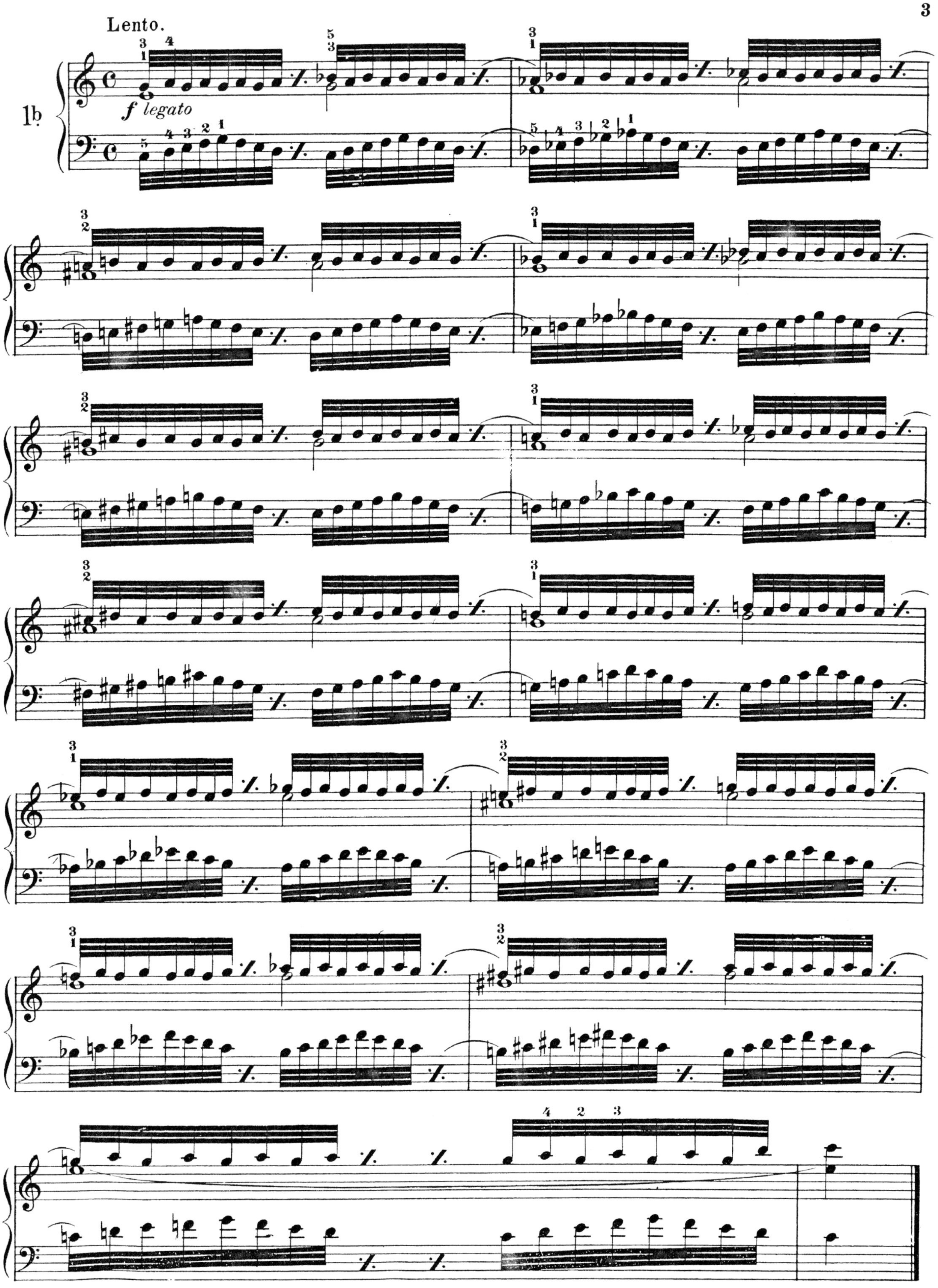
Lento.
1b
f legato

Preparatory Exercises to No. 2a

Practise in all keys.

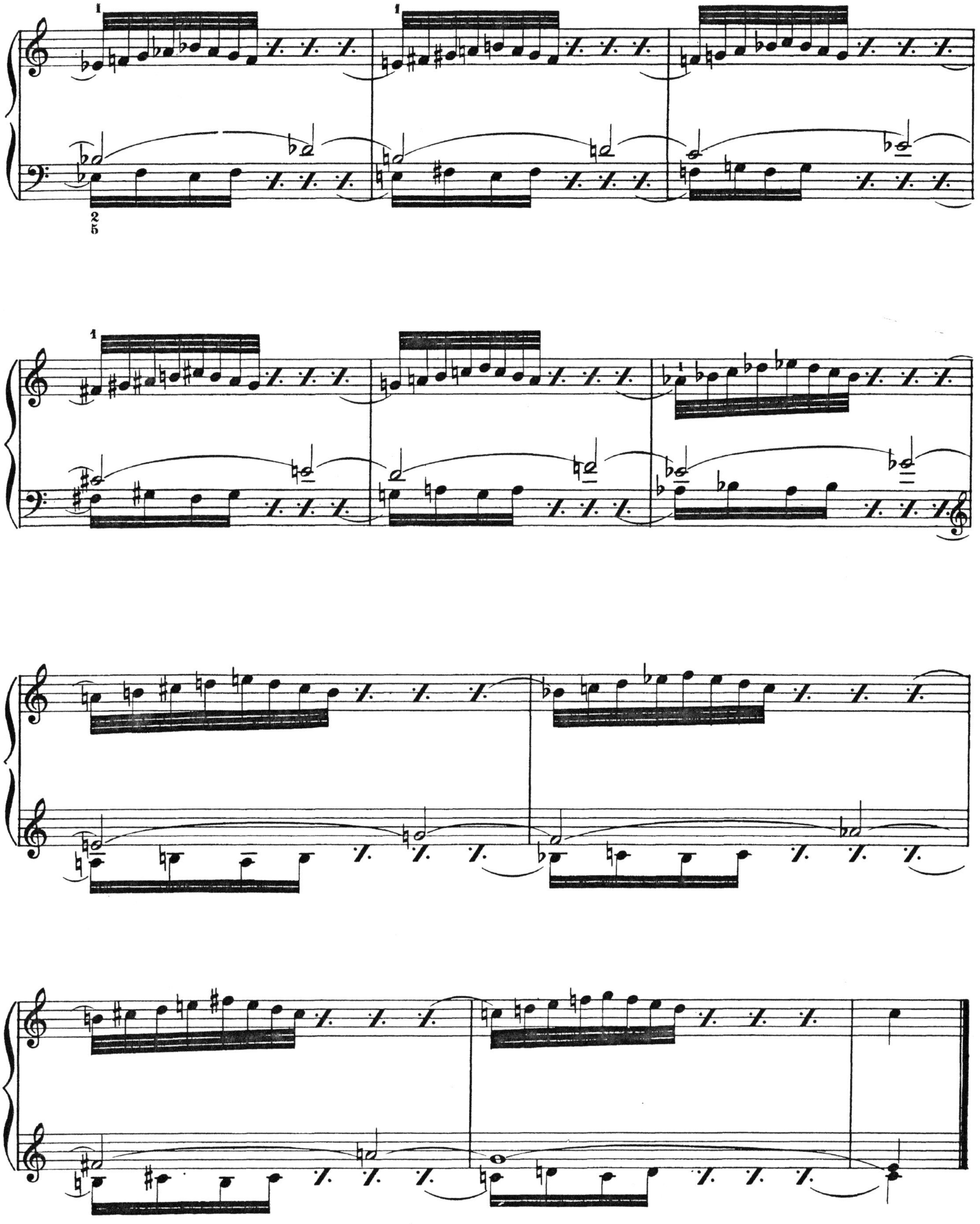

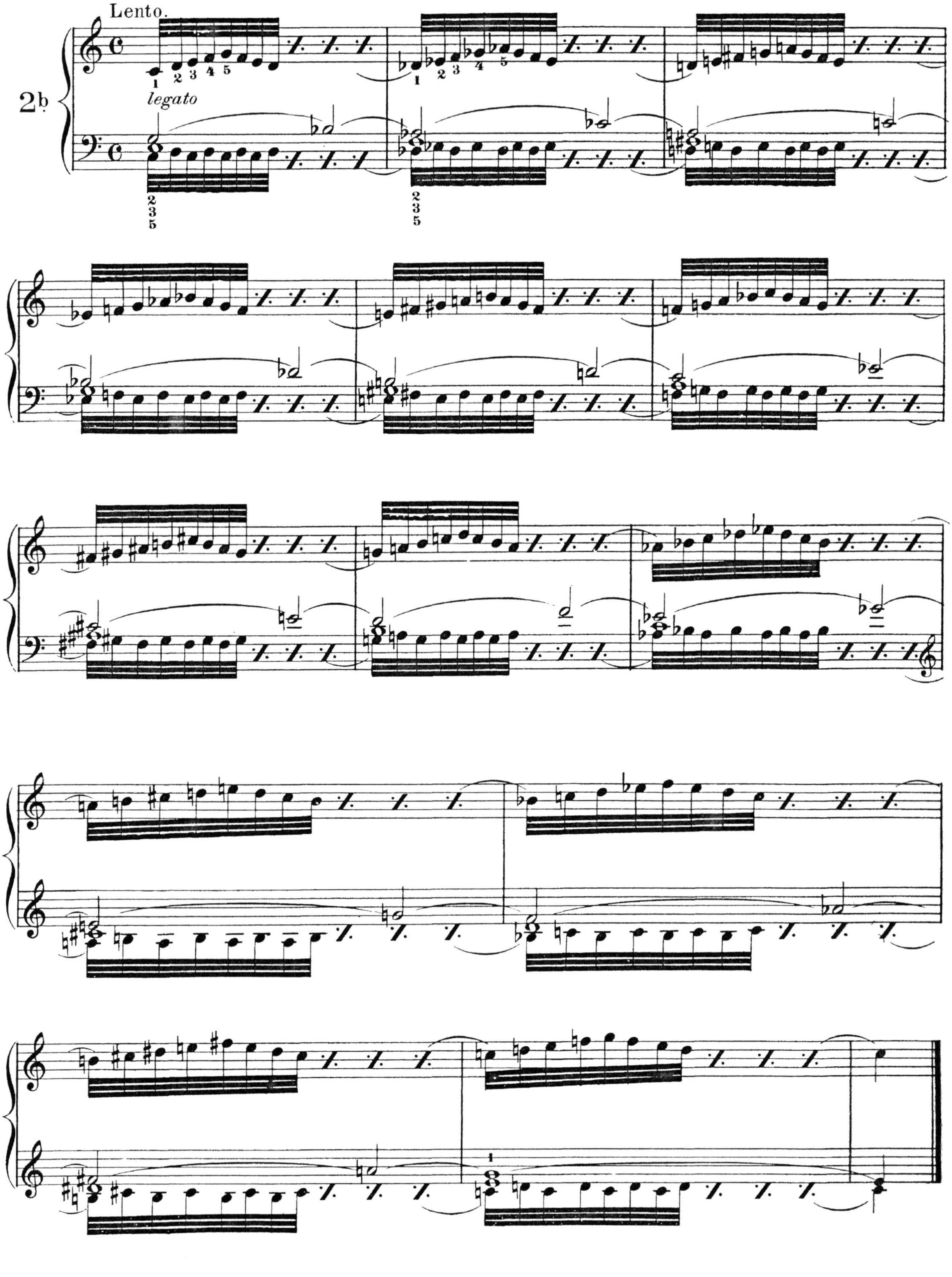
Lento.
2b
legato

Preparatory Exercises to Nº 3.

Practise in all keys.

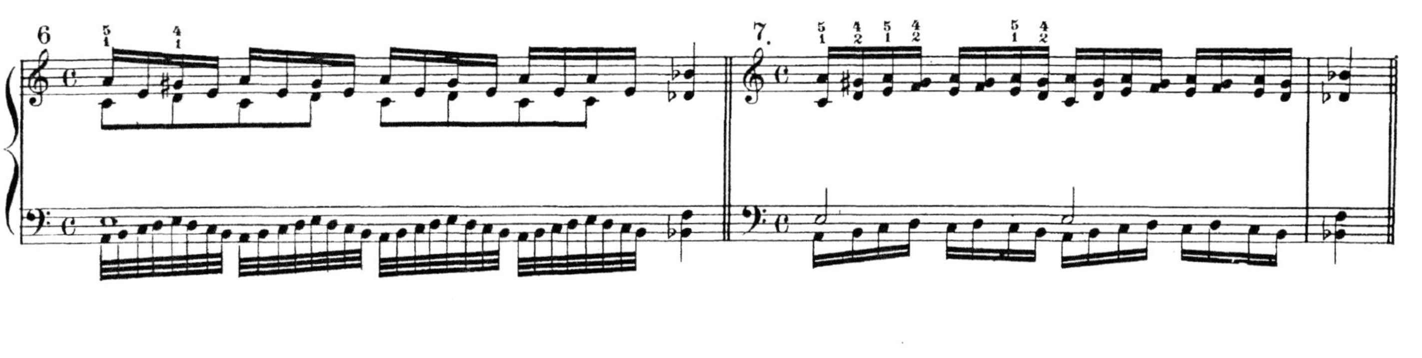

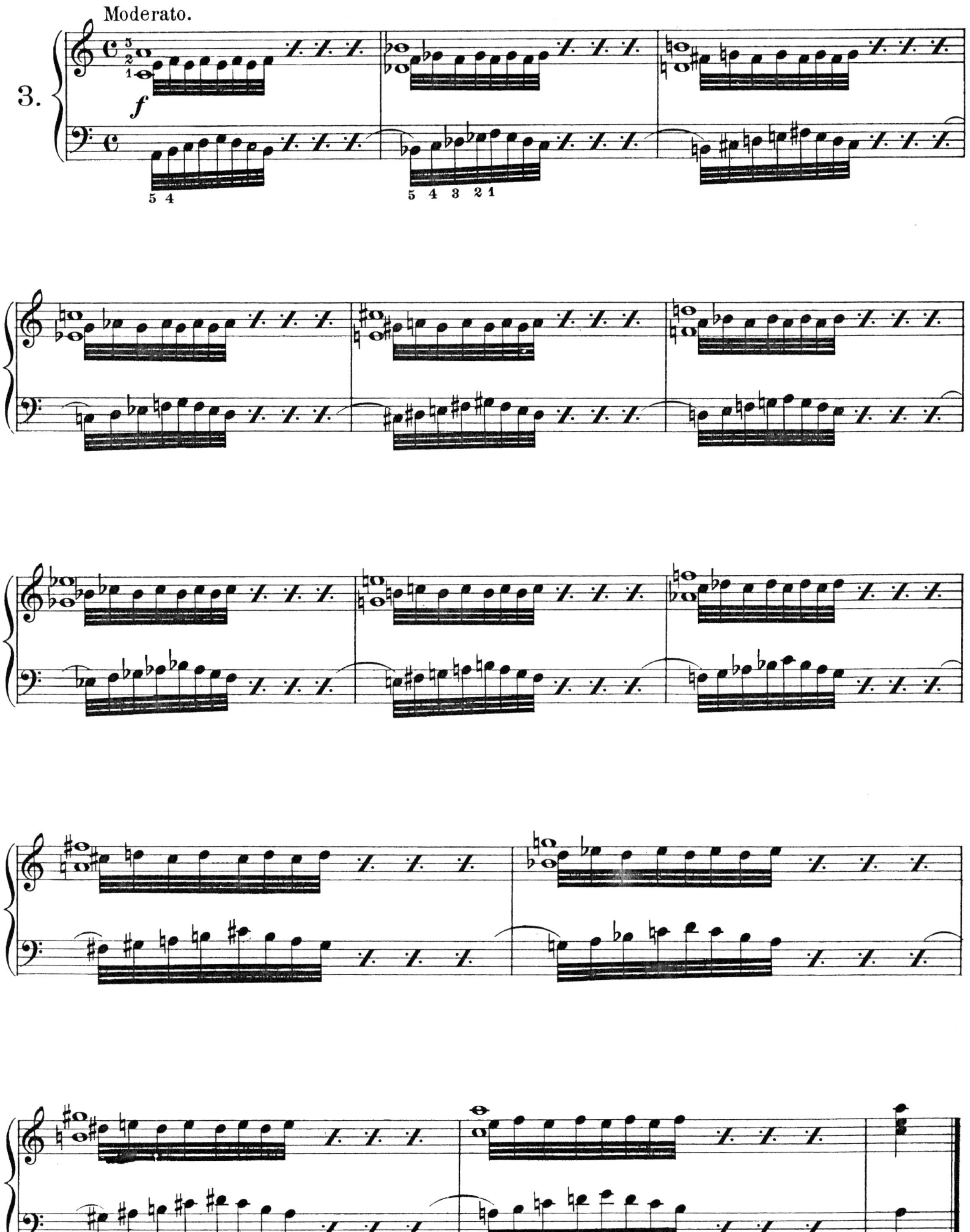
Moderato.
3.
f

Preparatory Exercises to Nº 4.

Practise in all keys.

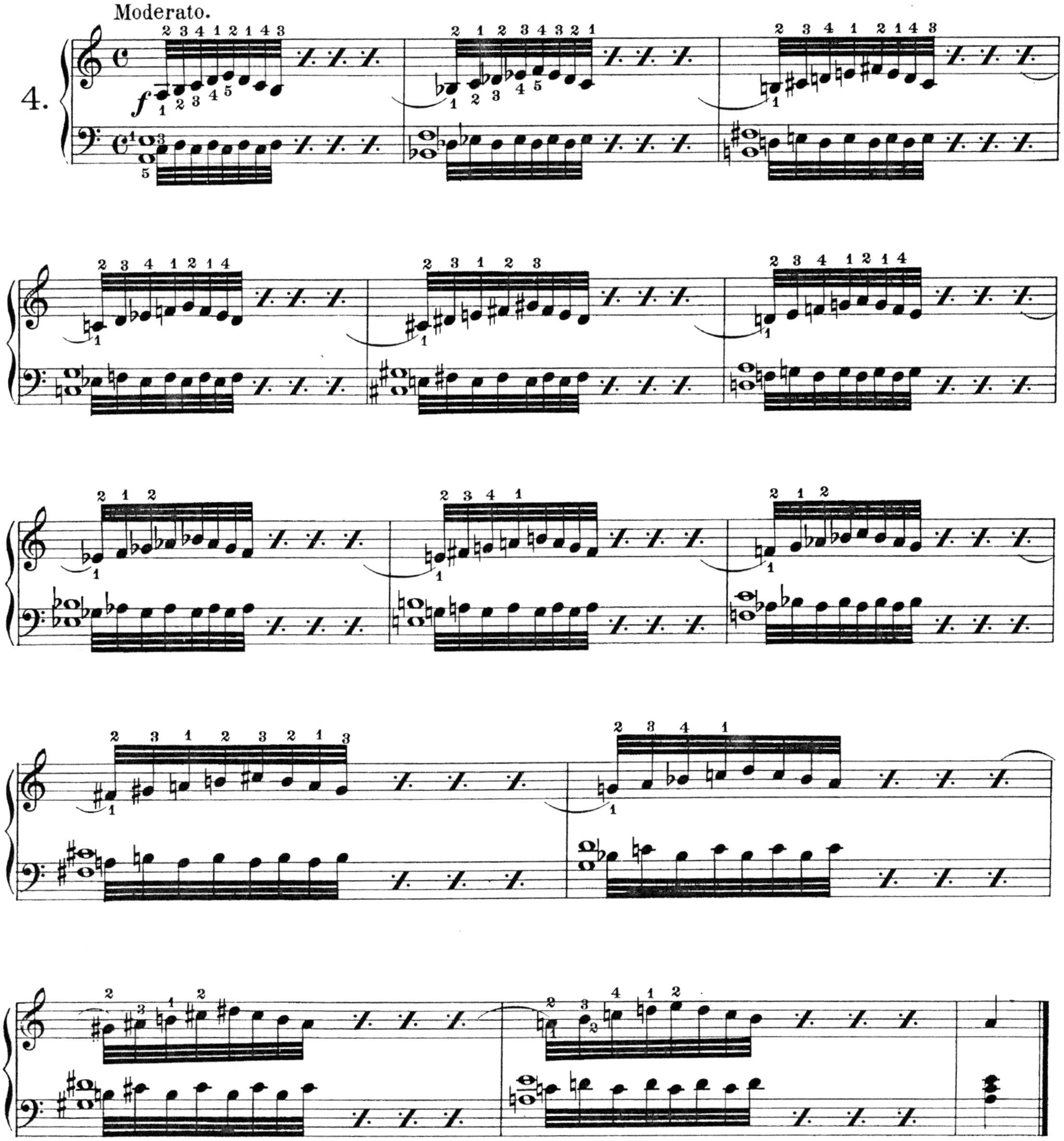

Preparatory Exercises to No. 5.

Practise in all keys.

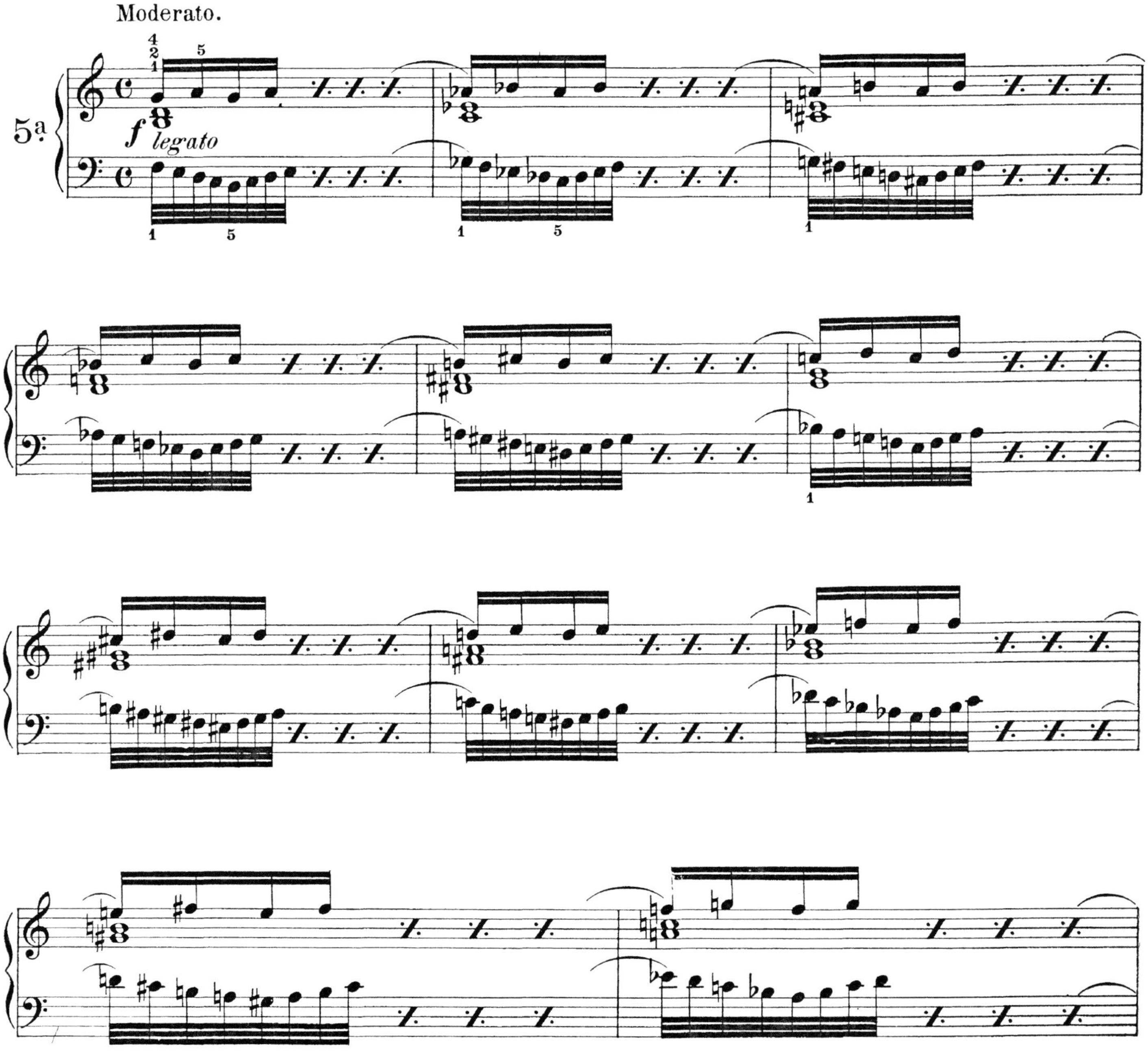

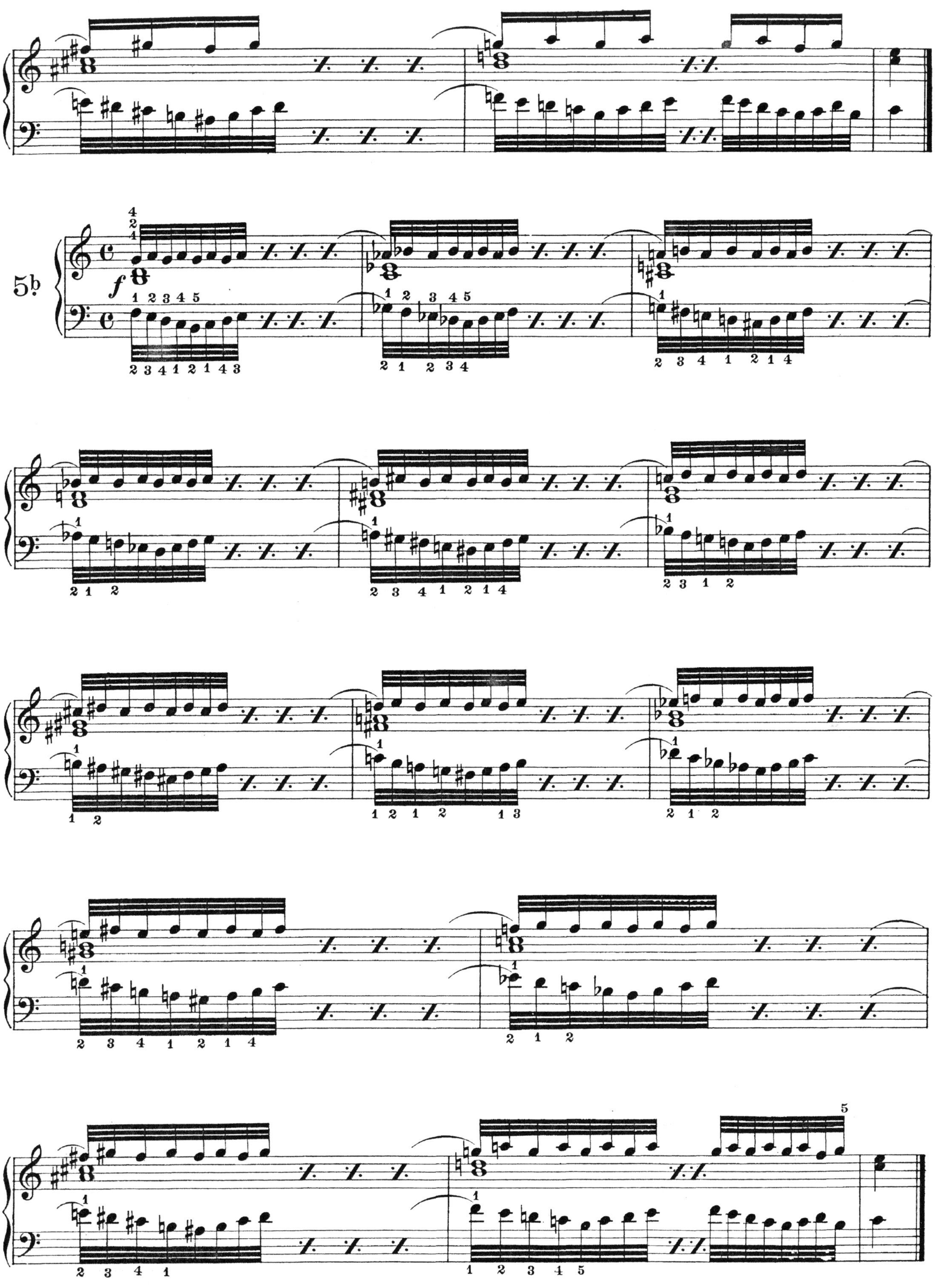
5♭

Preparatory Exercises to No. 6.

Practise in all keys.

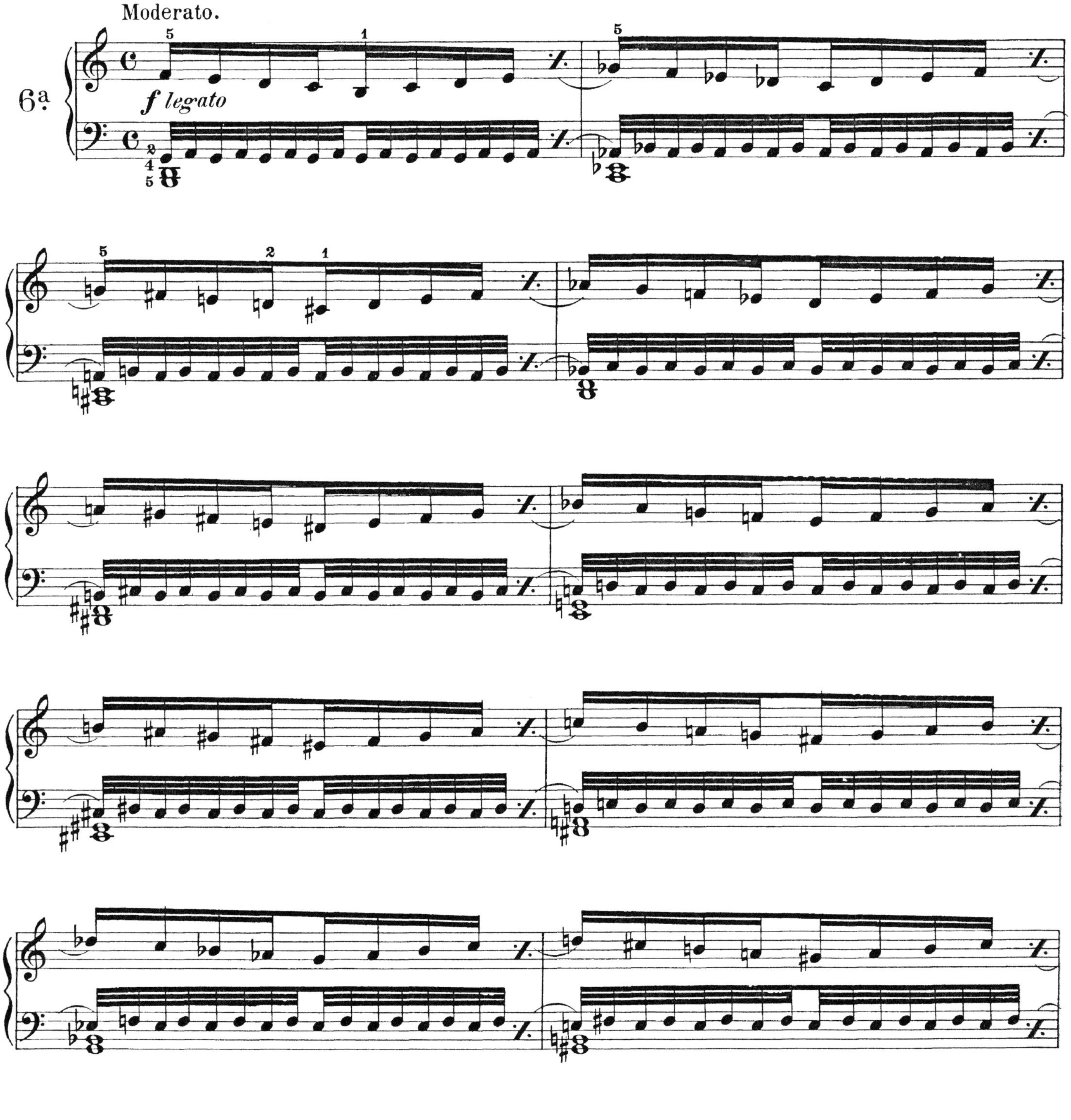

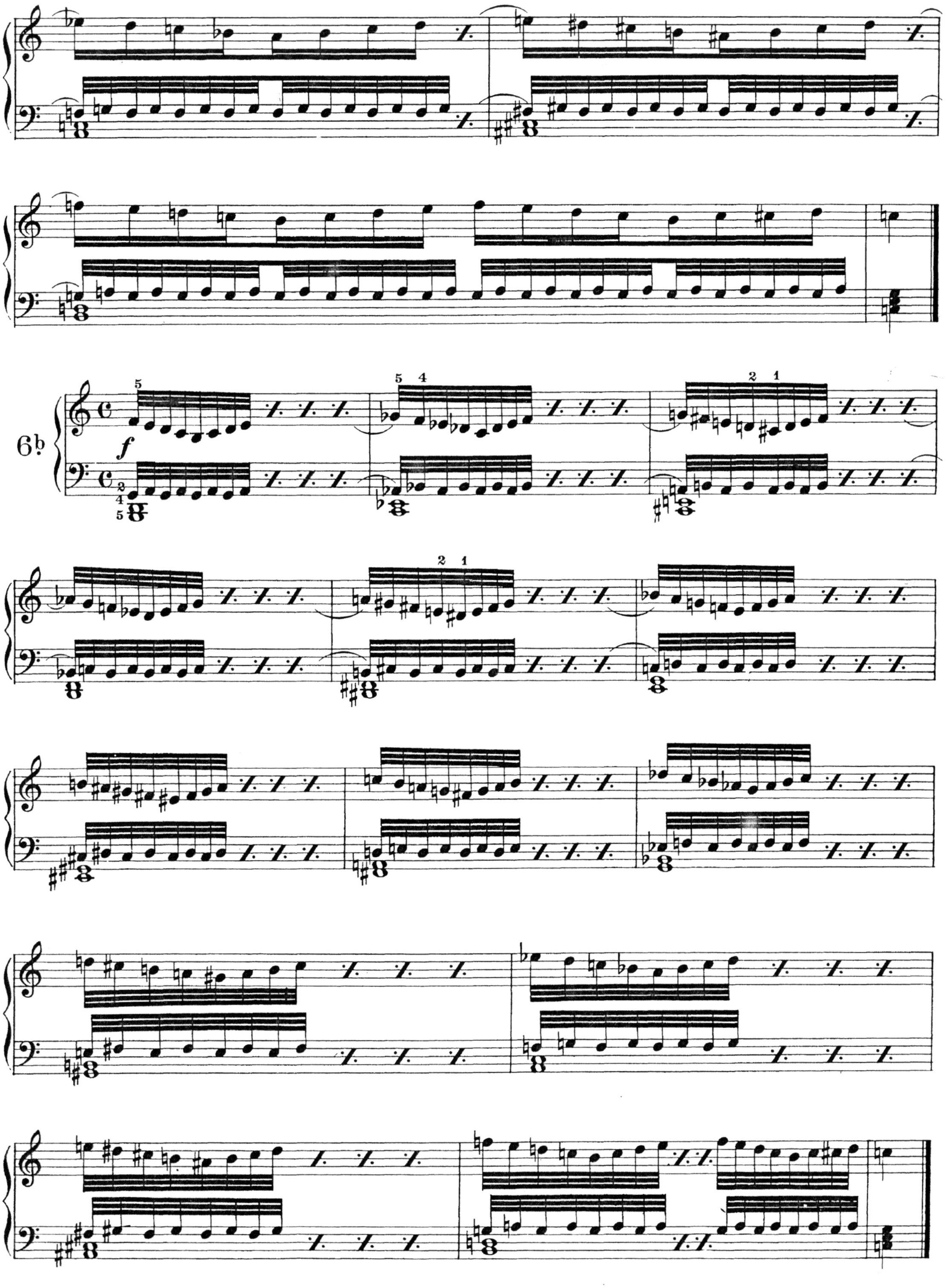
6b

Preparatory Exercises to Nº 7.

Practise in all keys.

Moderato.

Moderato.

7.

Preparatory Exercises to No. 8.

Practise in all keys.

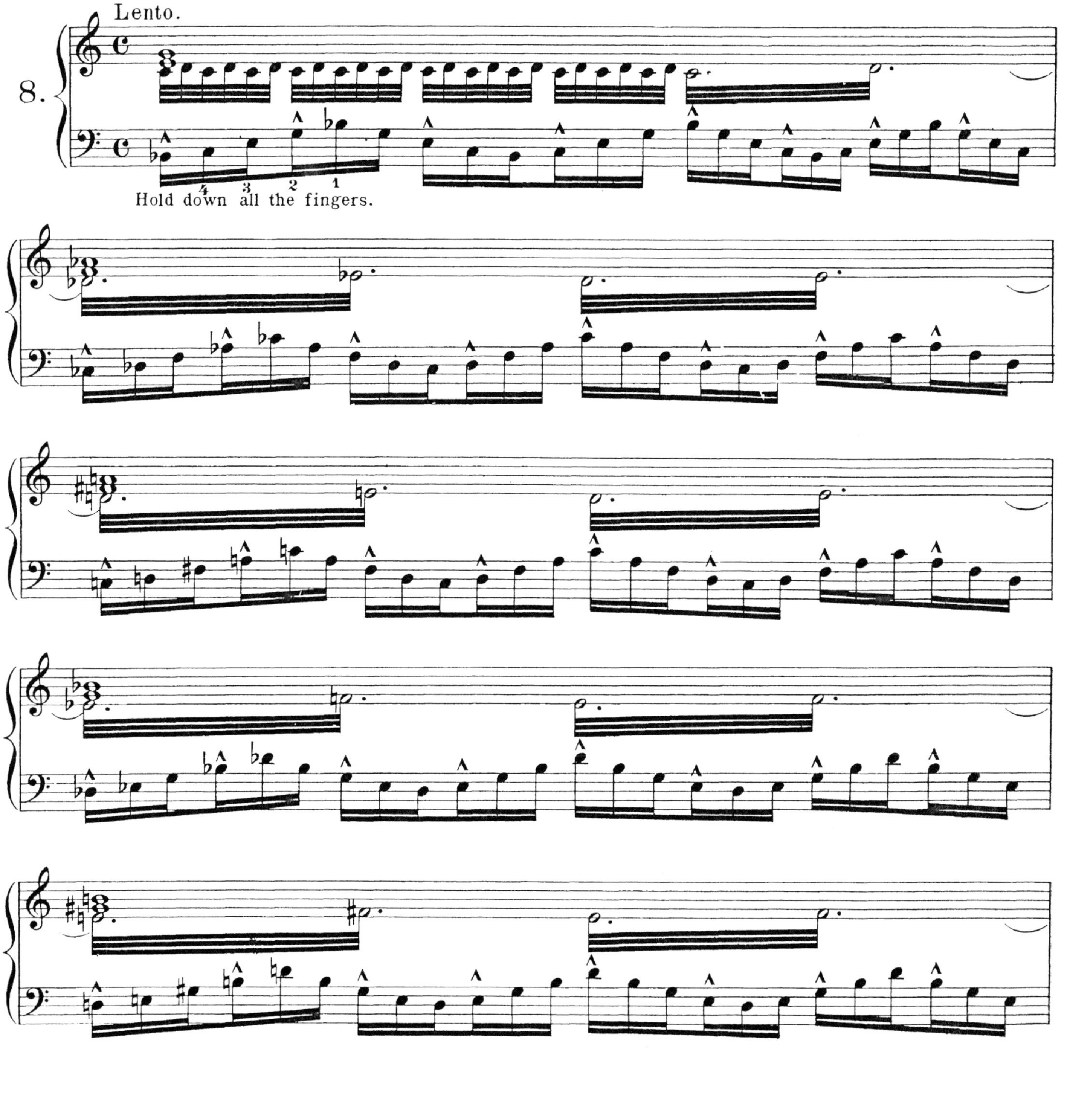

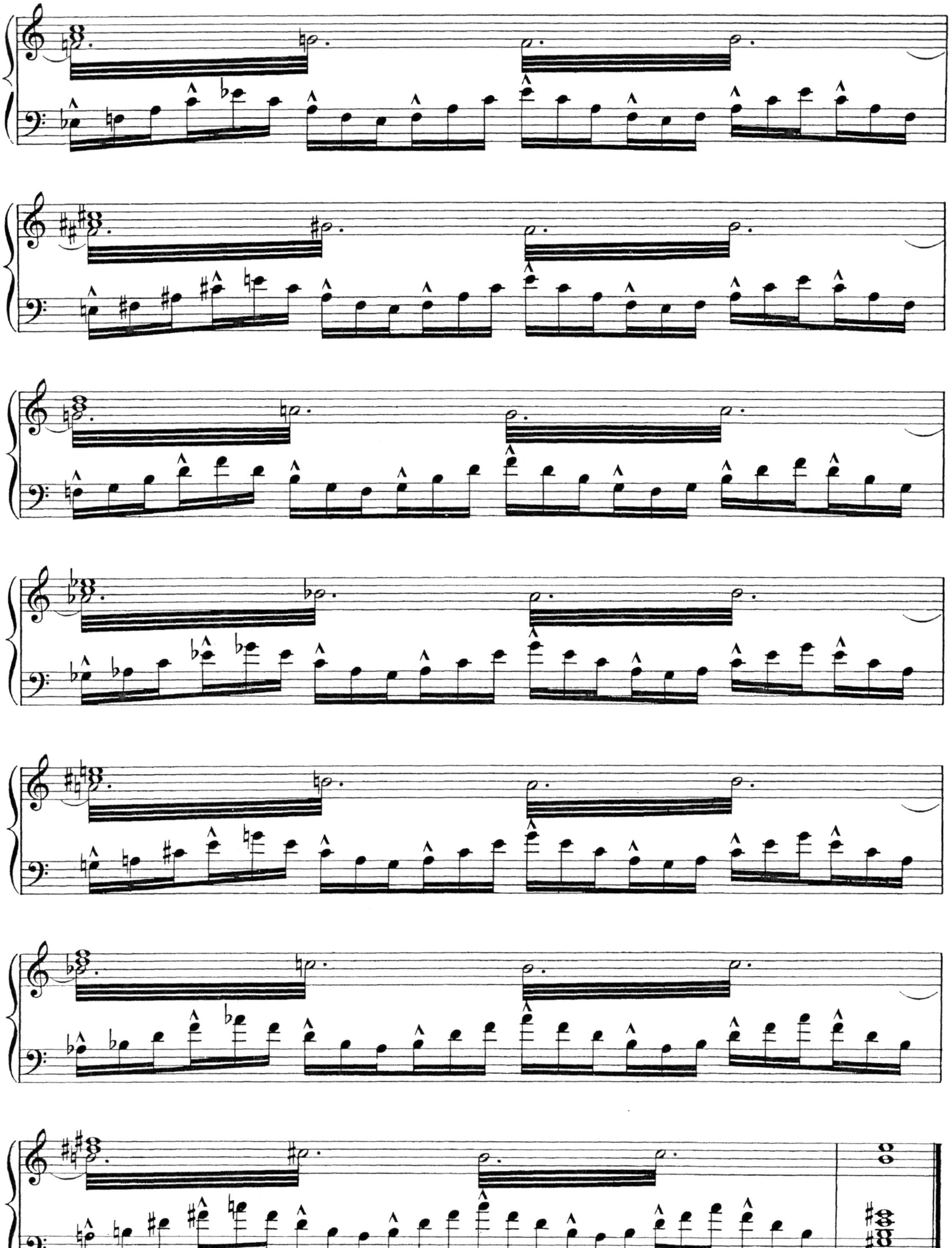

Preparatory Exercises to No. 9.

Practise in all keys.

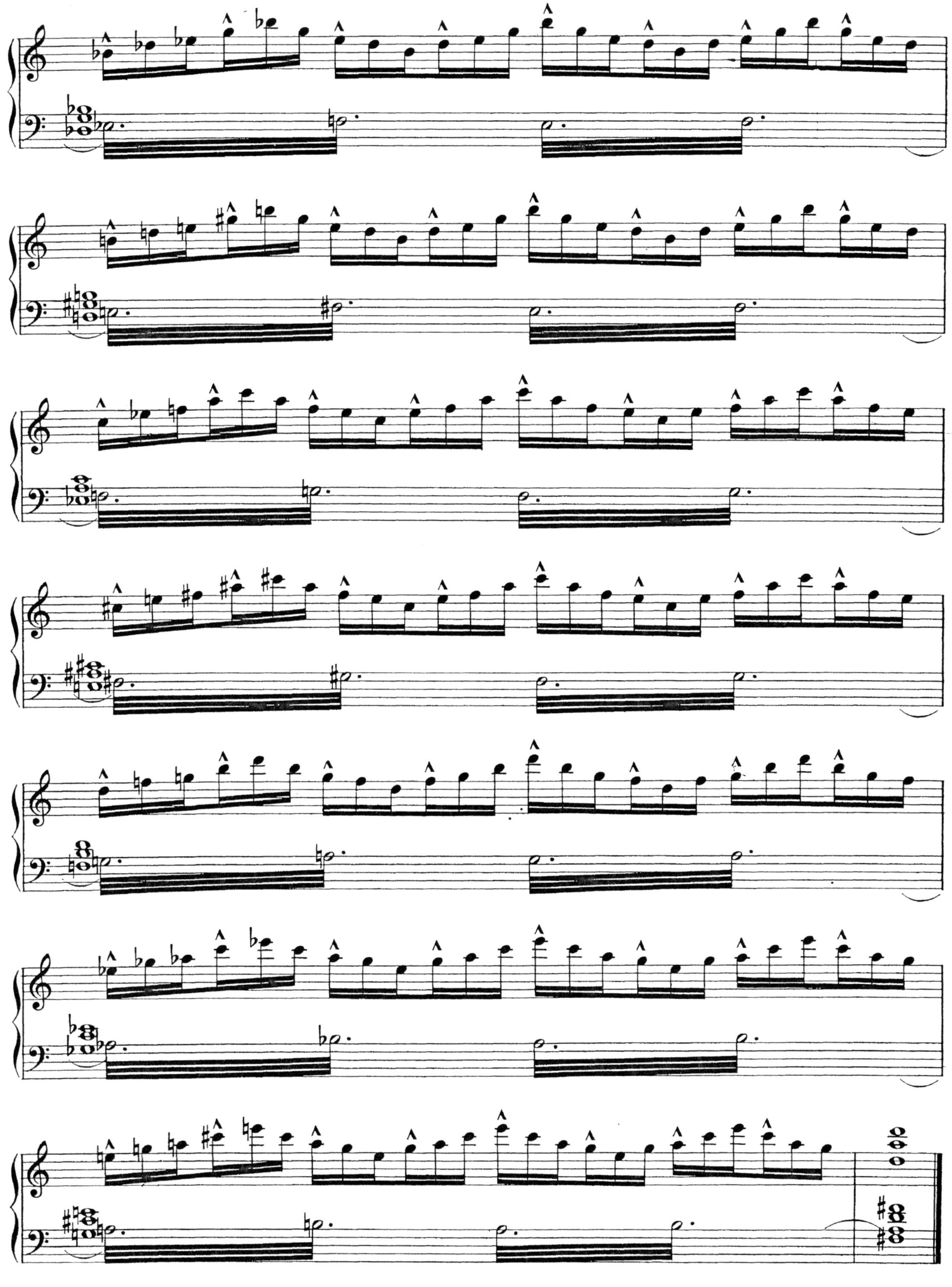

Lento.

10.

In all keys.

Preparatory Exercises to Nº 11.

Practise in all keys.

Left hand.

Lento.

Hold down all the fingers.

11.

Preparatory Exercises to Nº 12.

Practise in all keys.

Hold down all the fingers.

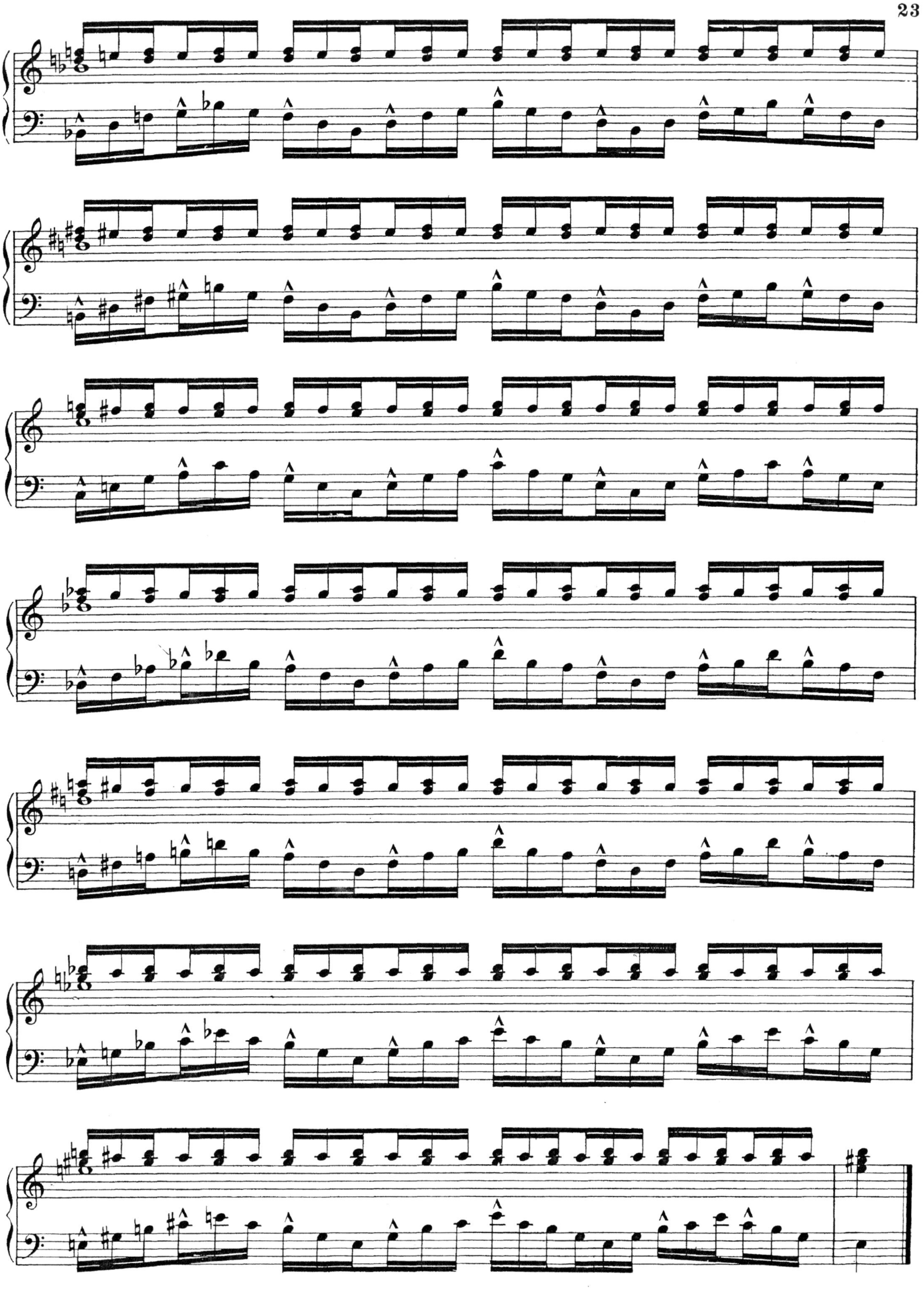

Preparatory Exercises to Nº 13.

Practise in all keys.

Lento.

Lento.

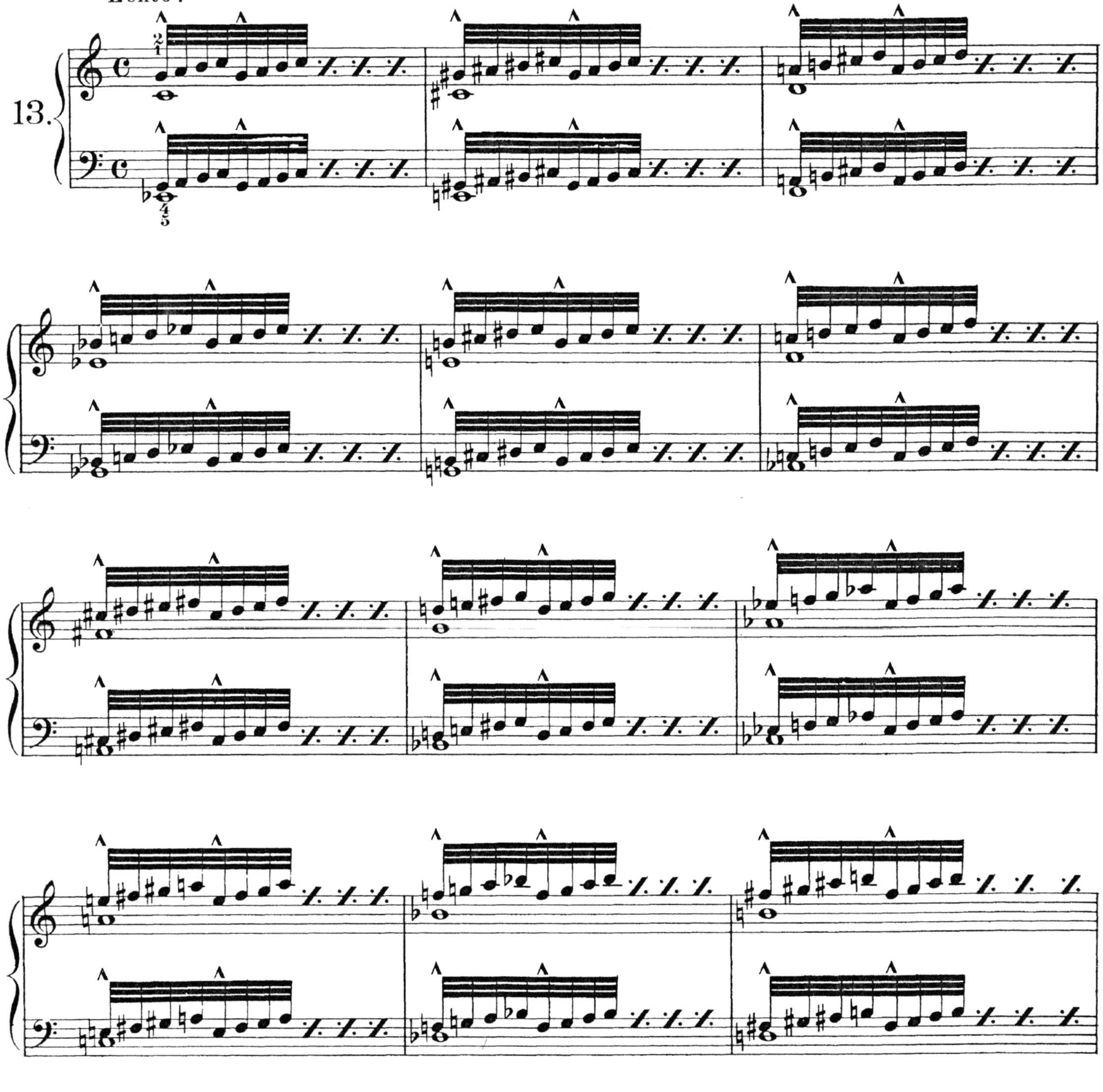

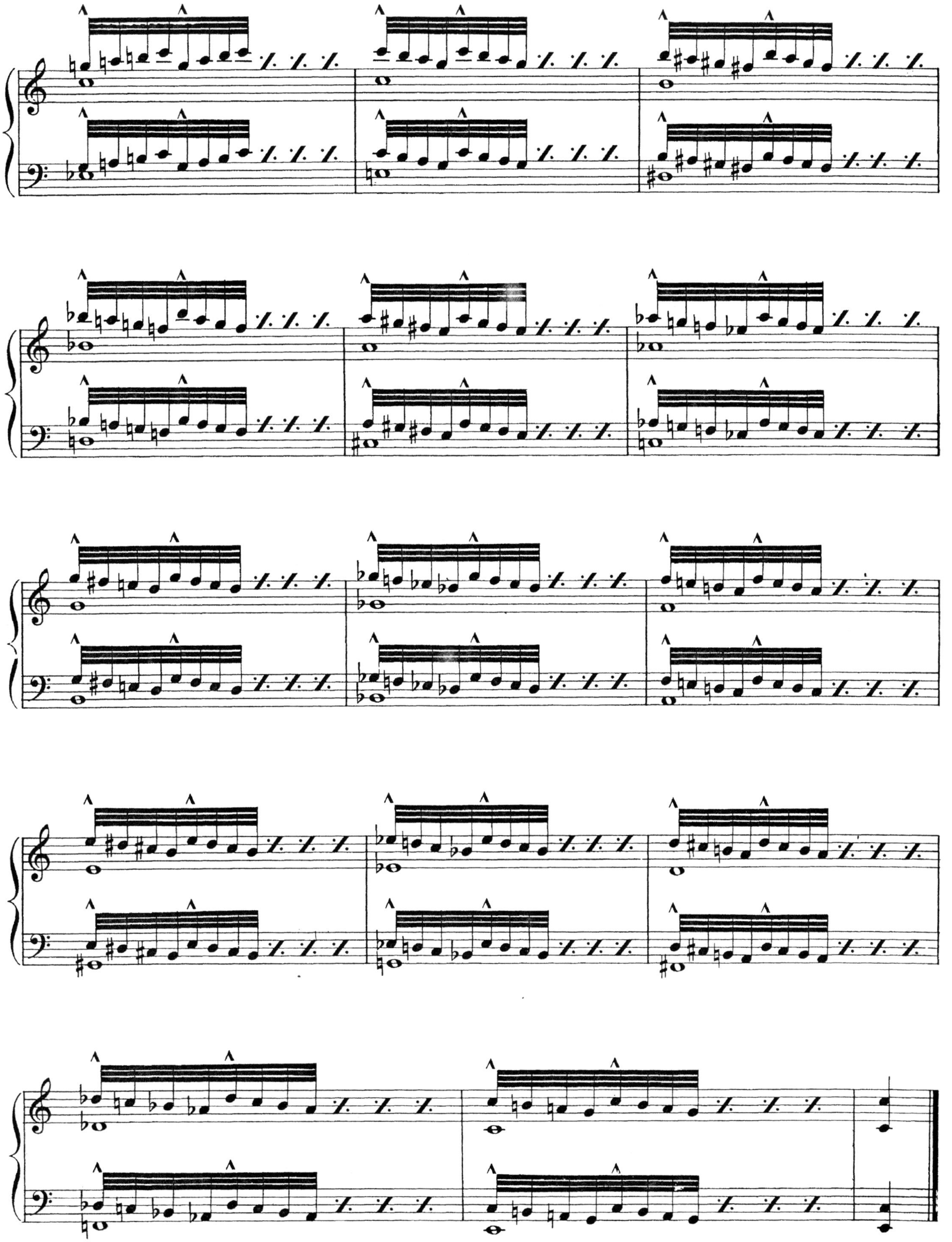

Preparatory Exercises to No. 14.

Practise in all keys.

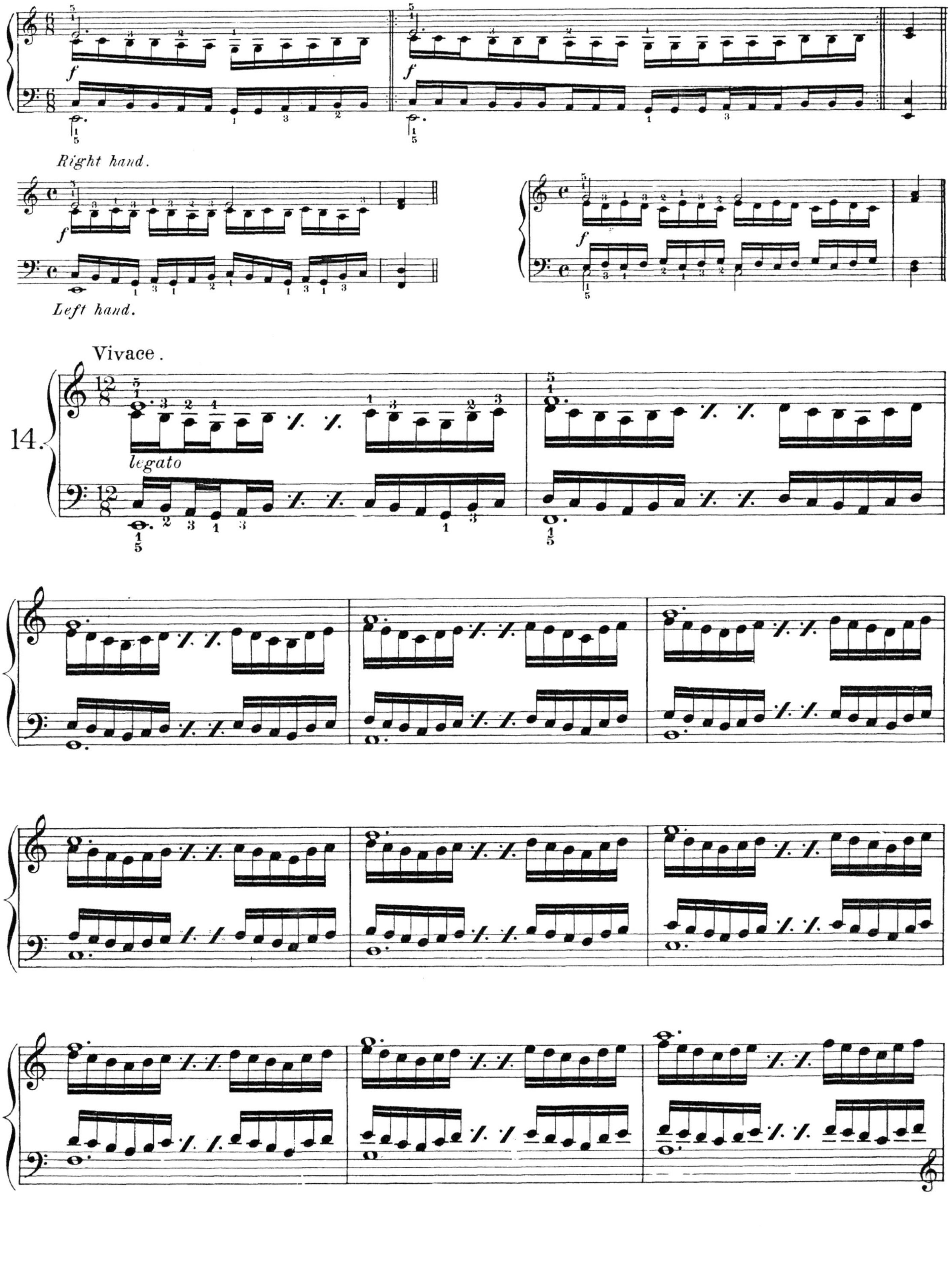

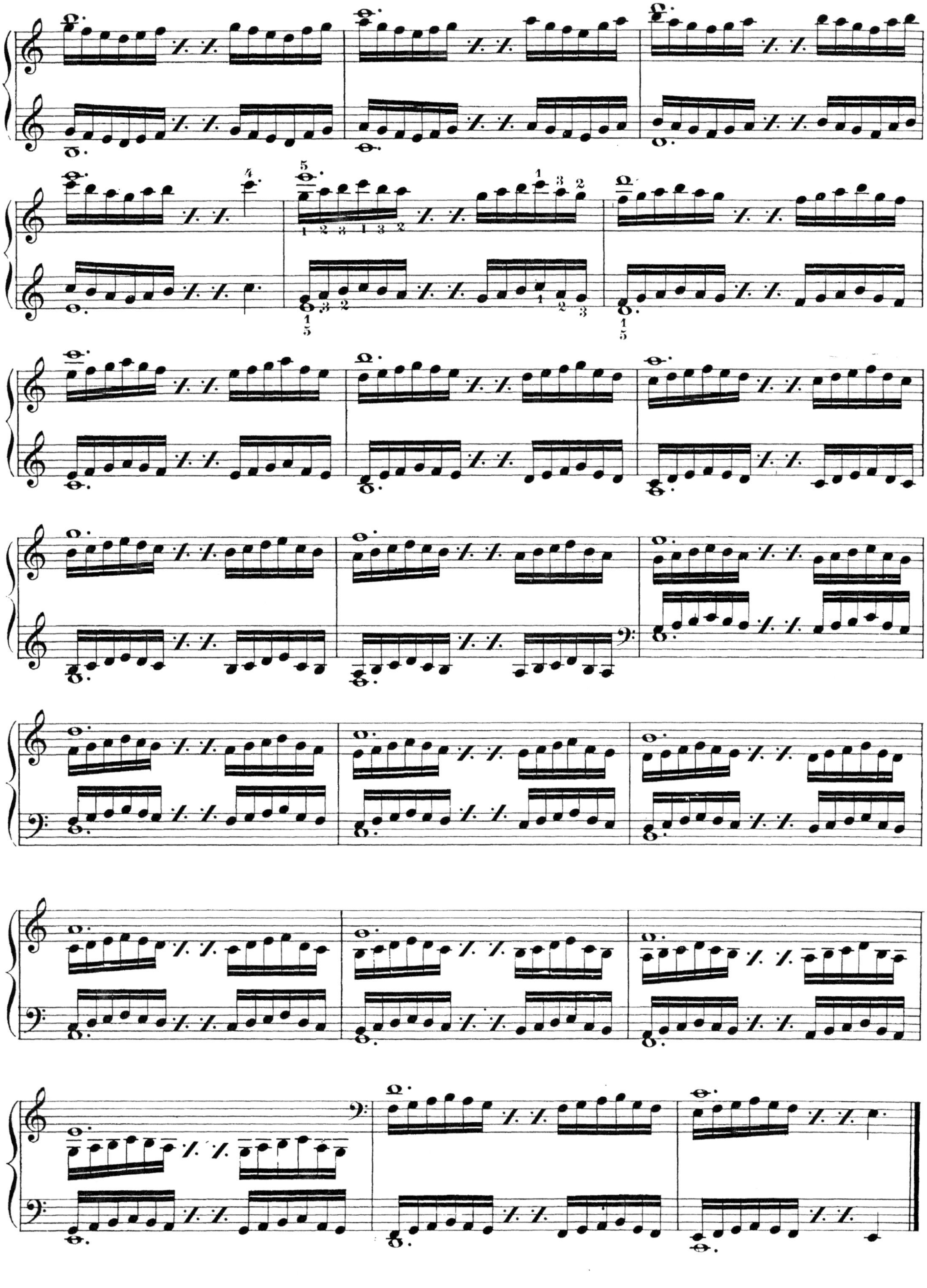

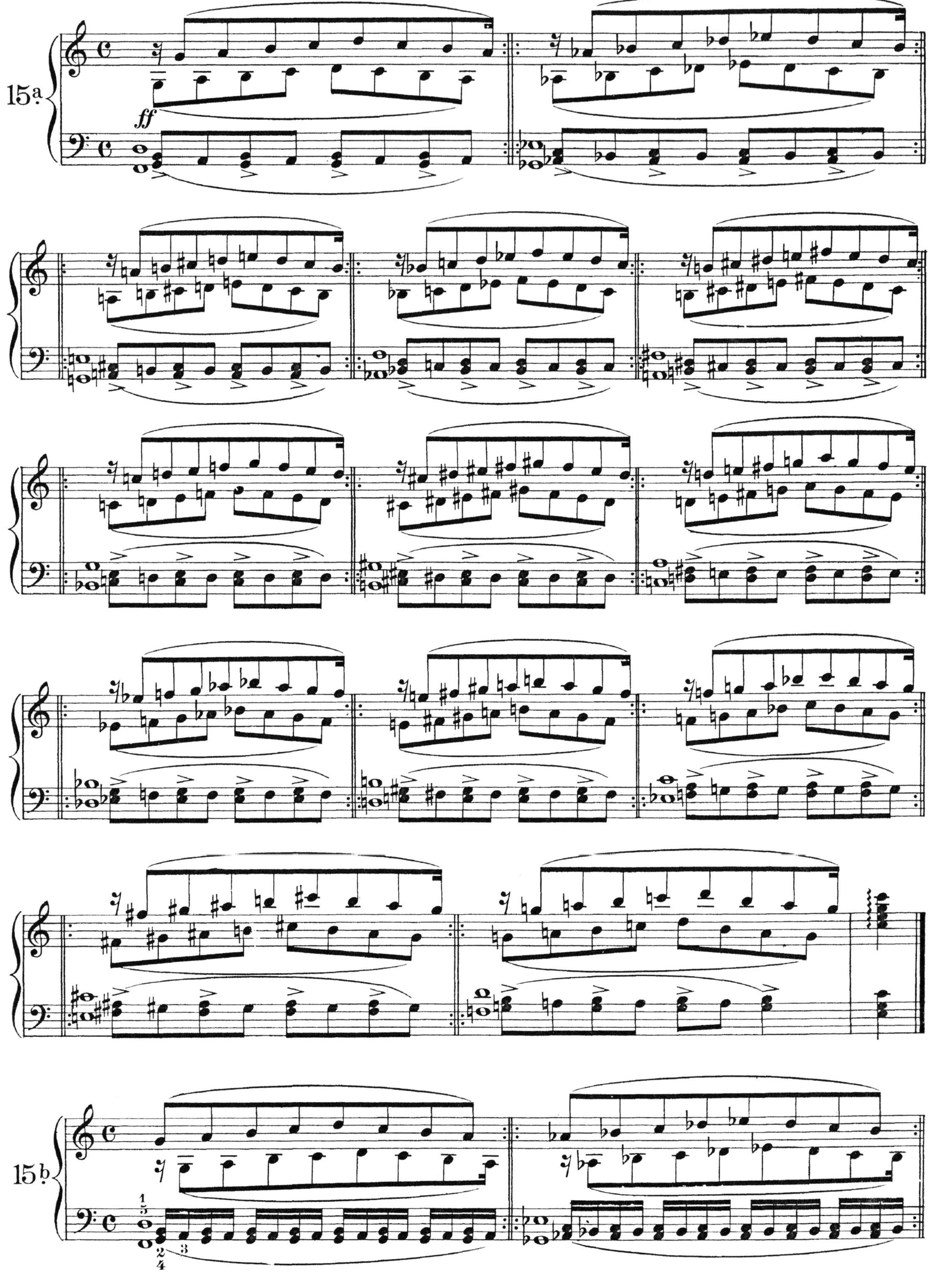
15a.
ff
15b.

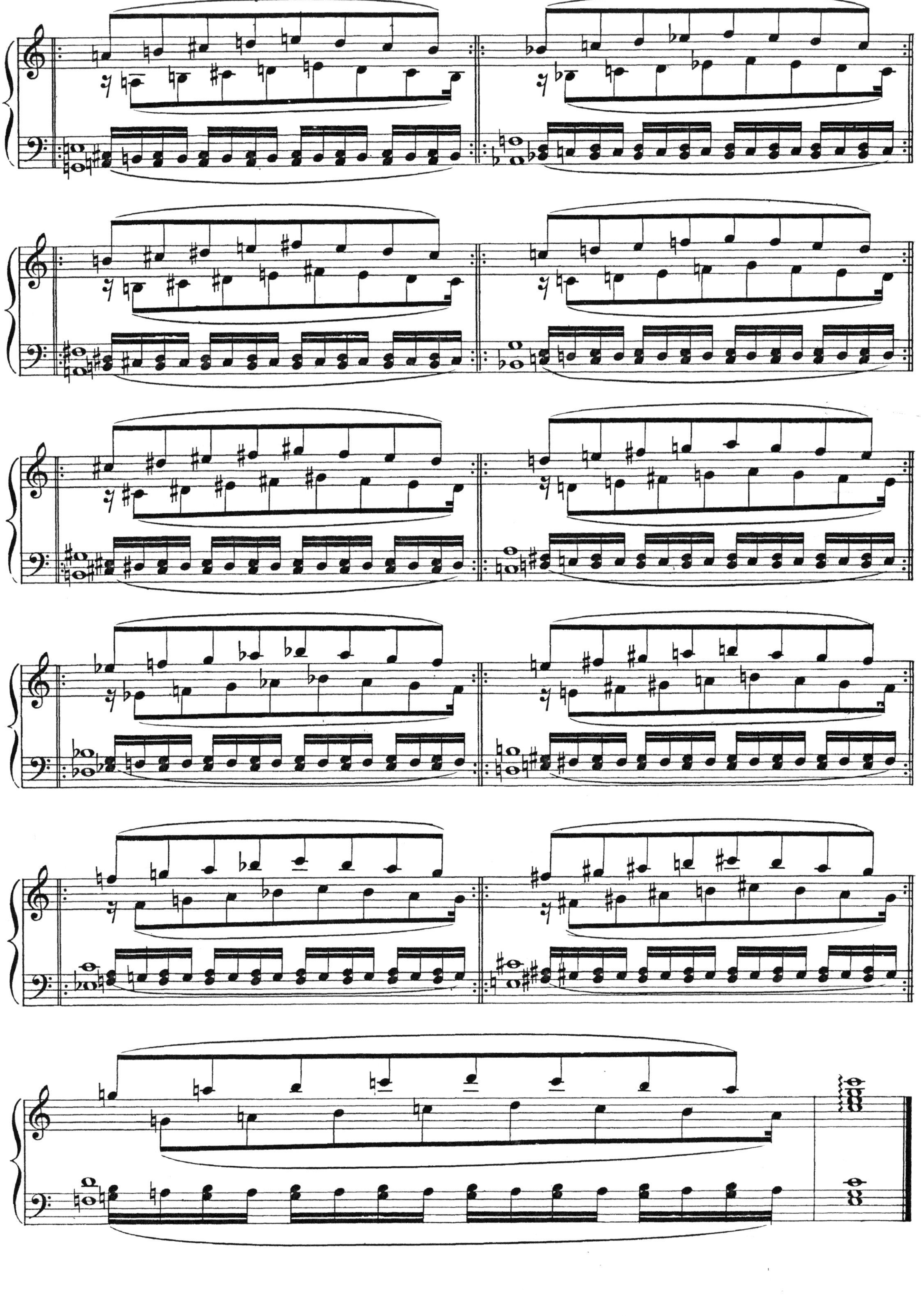

Preparatory Exercises to Nº 16ª

Practise in all keys.

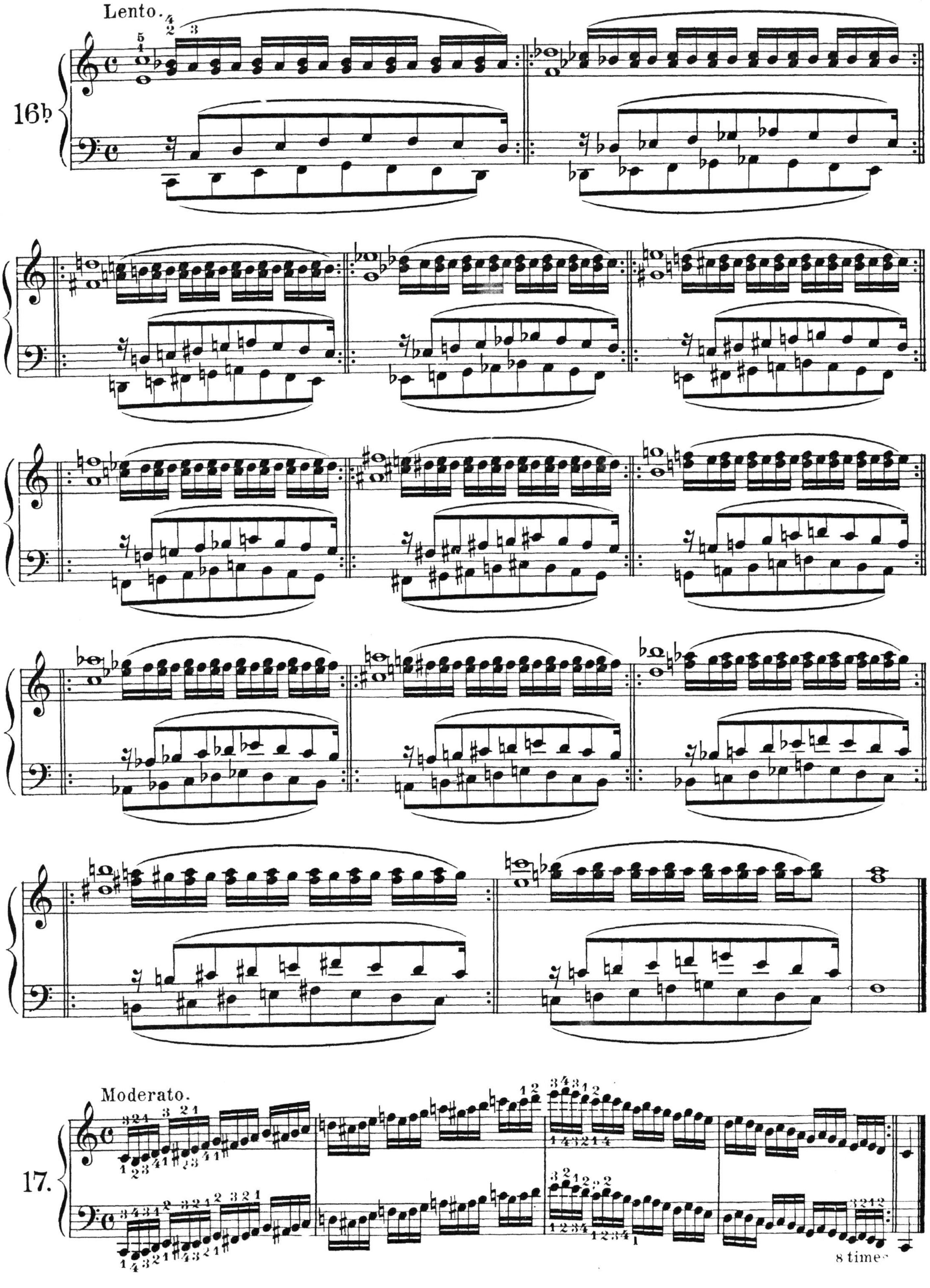
Lento.
16b
Moderato.
17.
8 times

Preparatory Exercises to Nº 19.

Practise in all keys.

Veloce.
20a
f
Veloce.
20b
f
8 times.

Preparatory Exercises to № 21.

Practise in all keys.

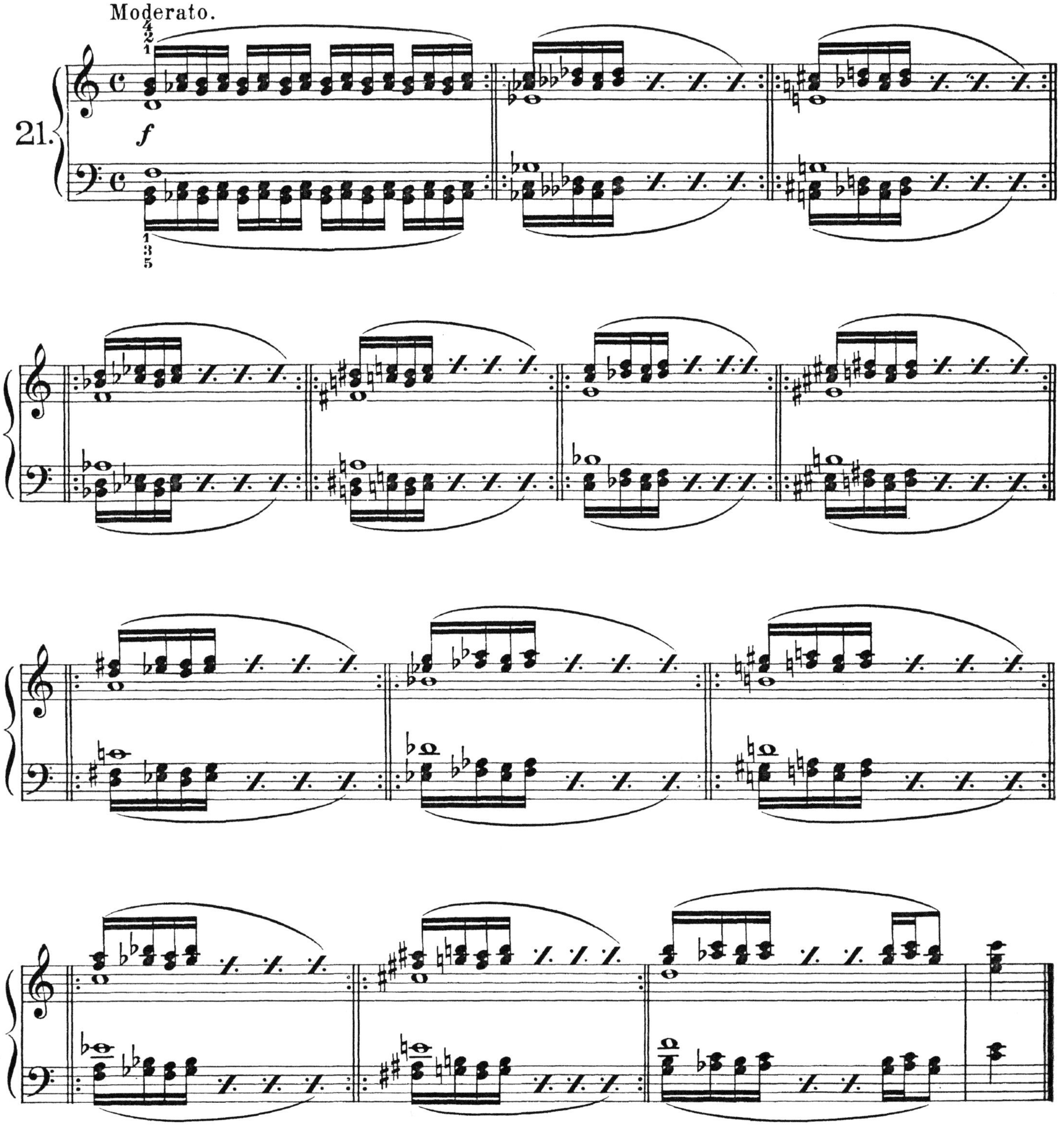

Moderato.

22.

Moderato.

23.

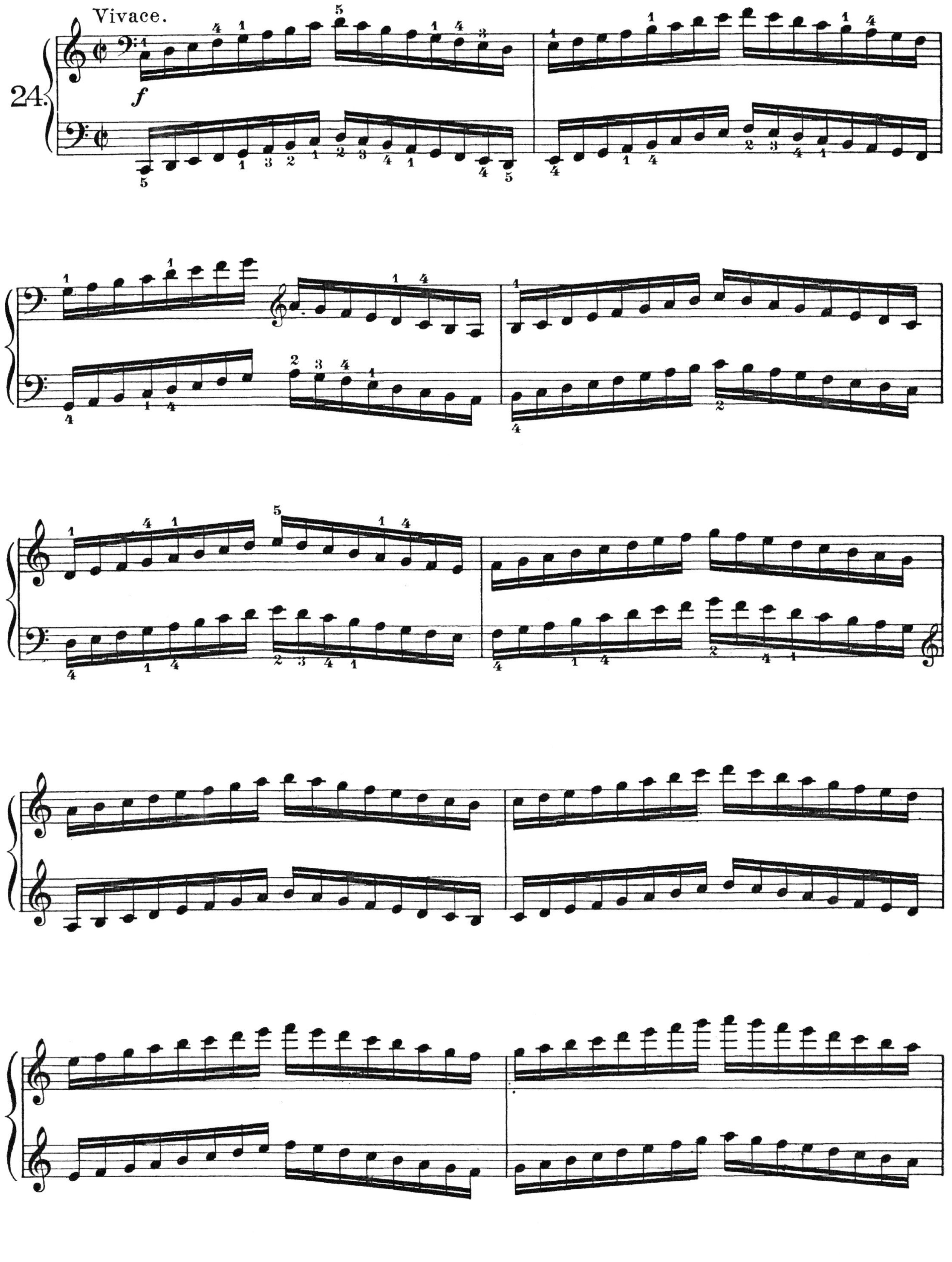
24.
Vivace.
f

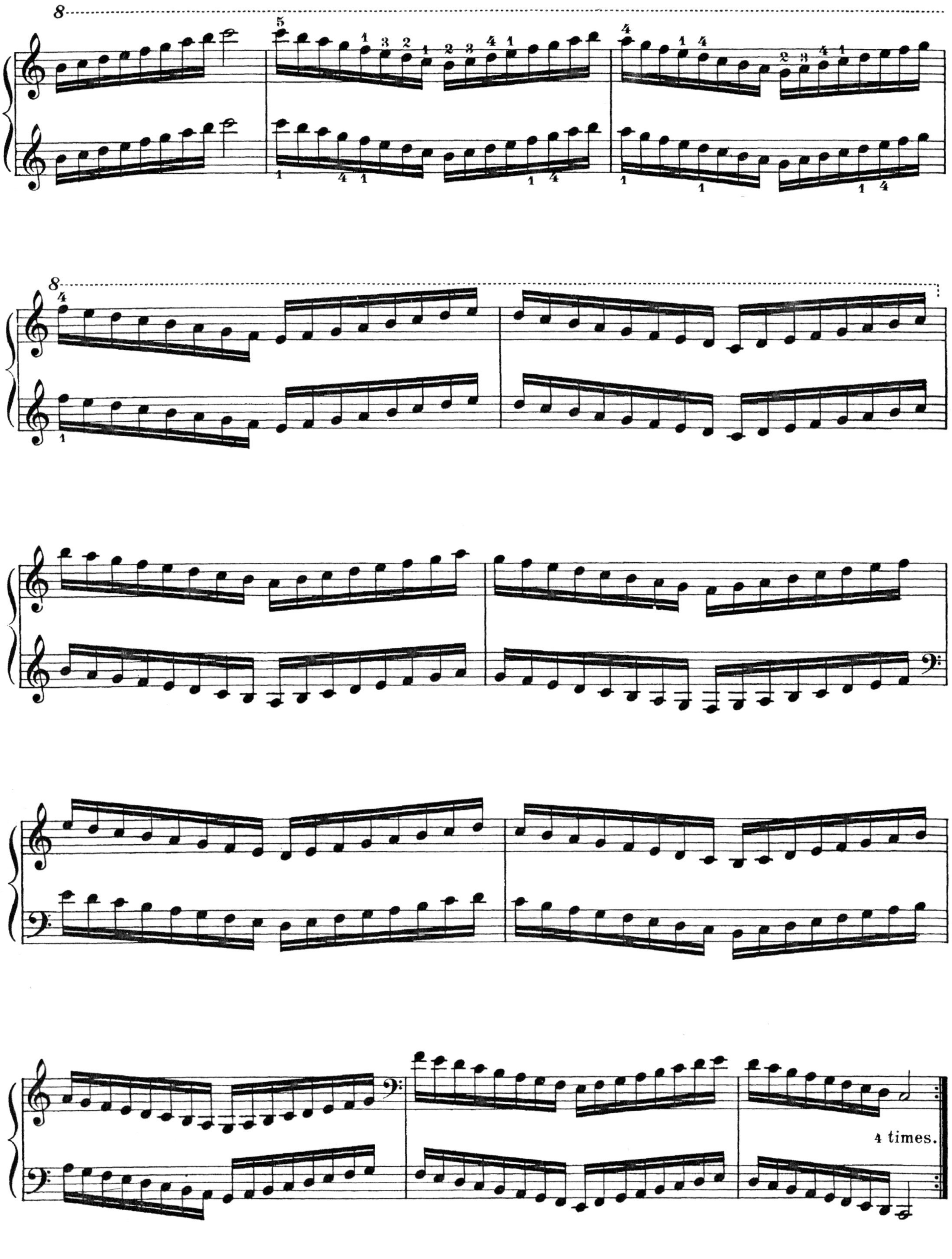
4 times.

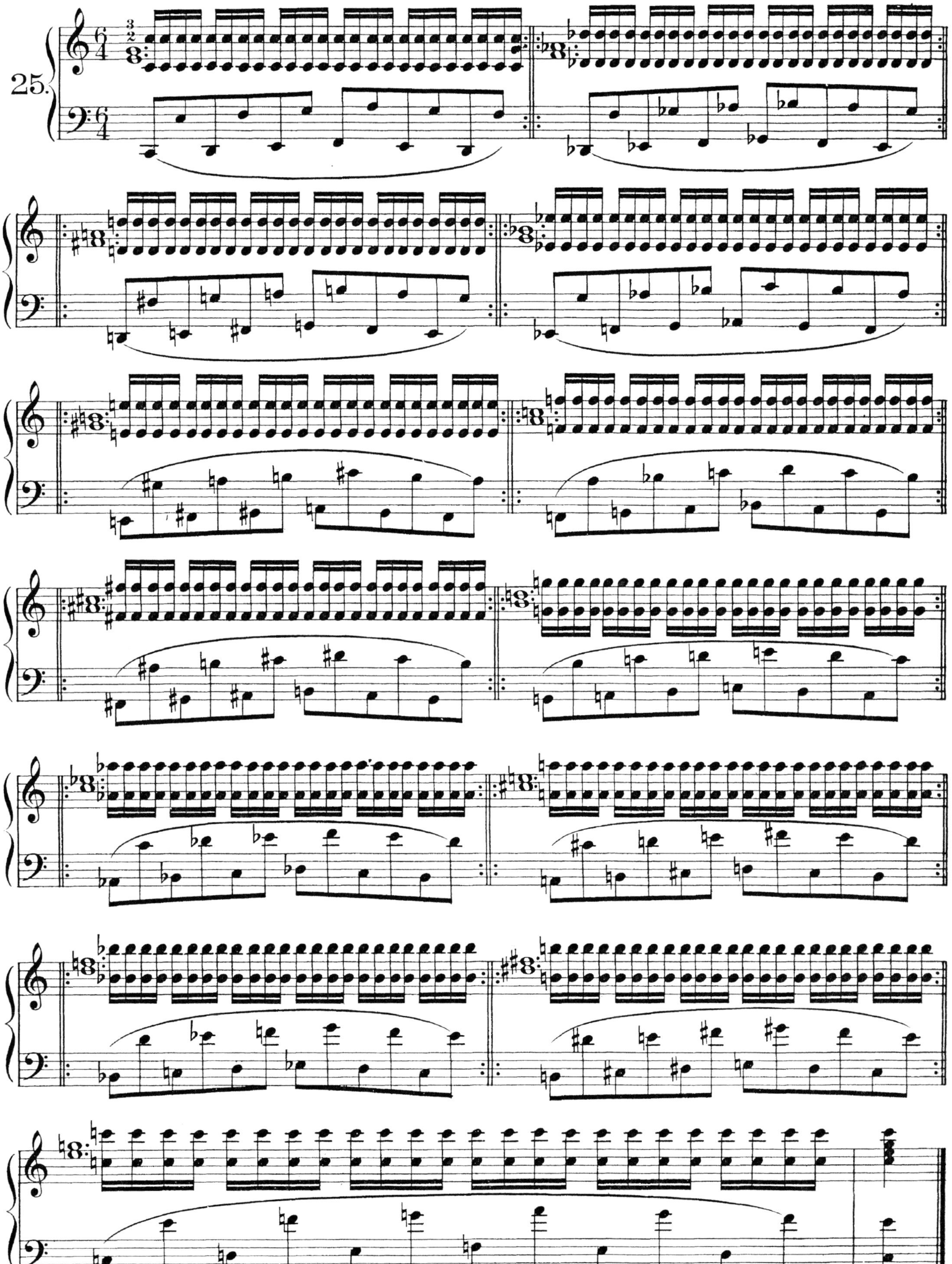
25.

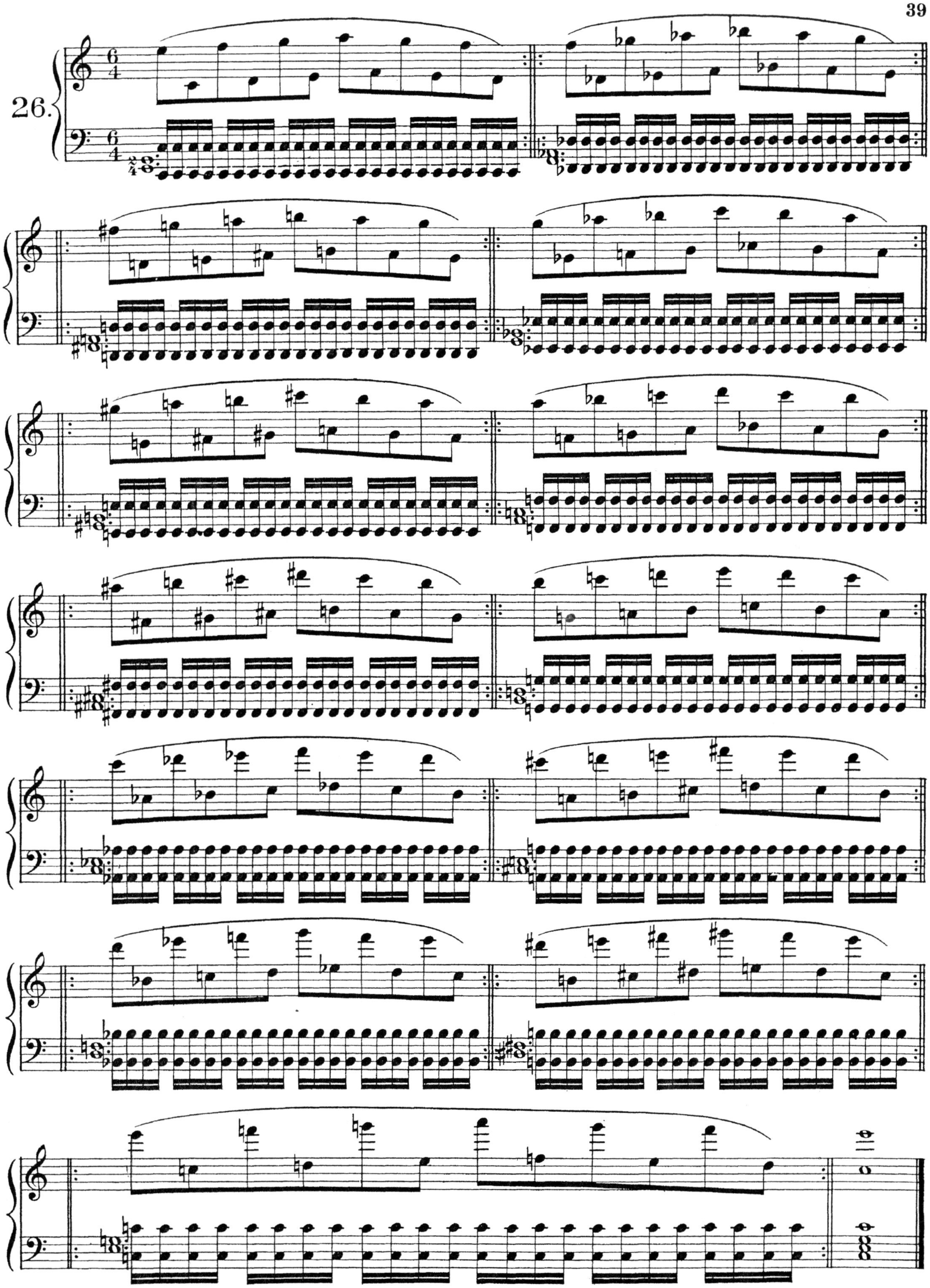
26.

Preparatory Exercises to No. 27.

Practise in all keys.

1.

2.

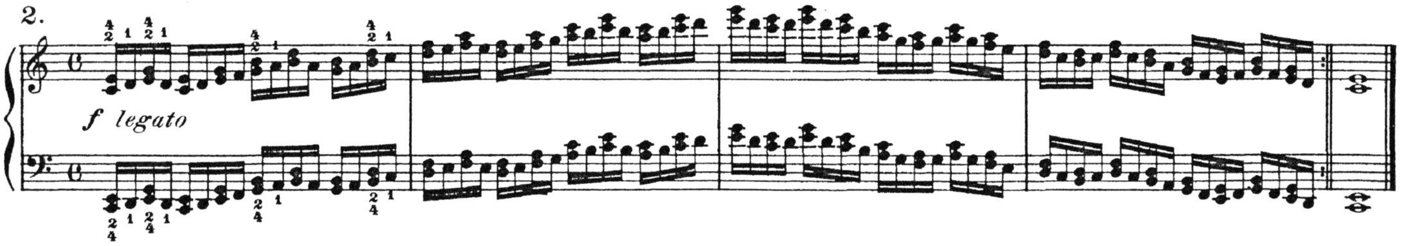

3.

27.

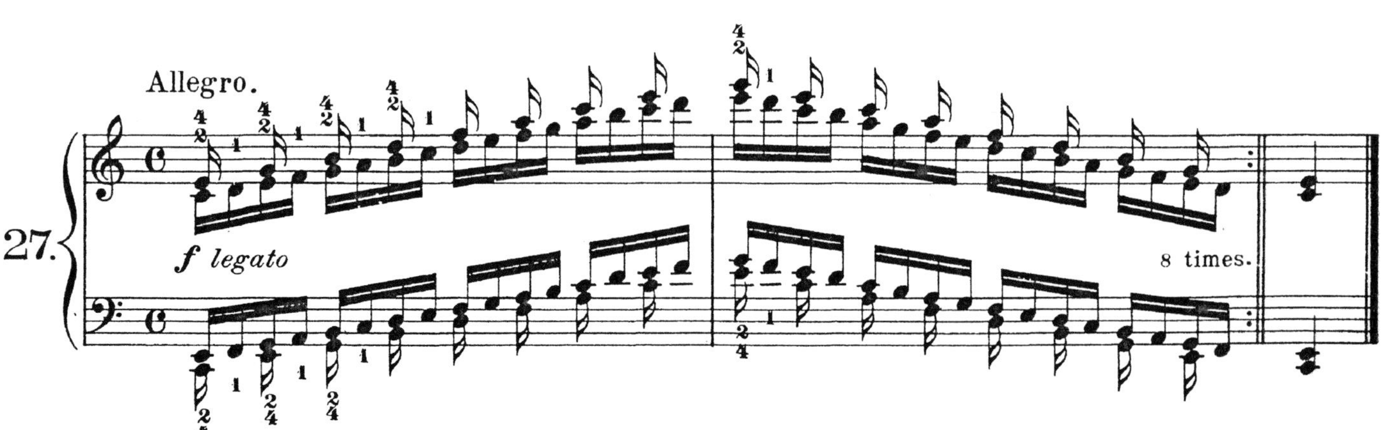

Preparatory Exercises to Nº 28.

Practise in all keys.

1. Veloce.

2.

Veloce.

28.

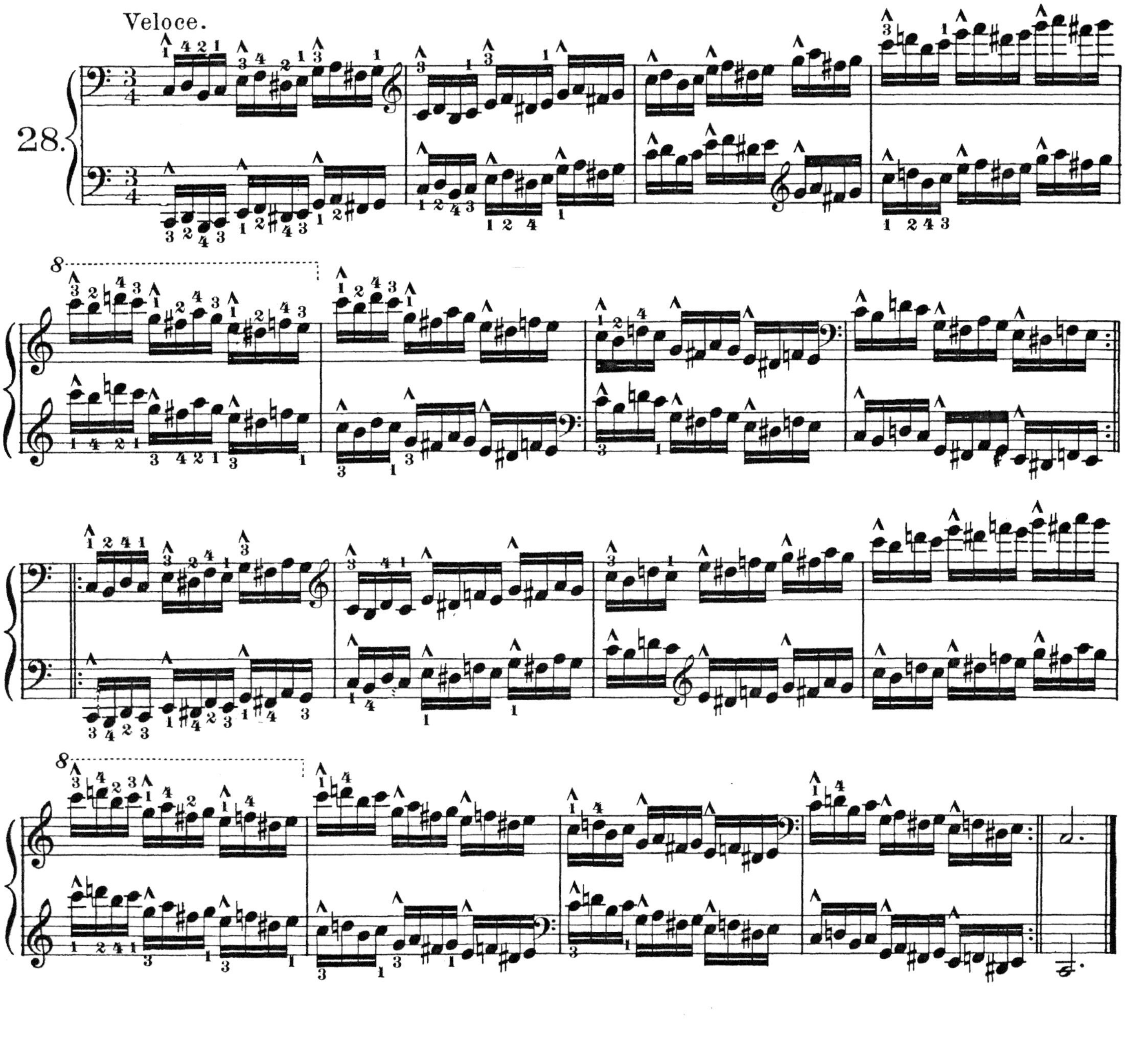

Preparatory Exercises to No. 29.

Practise in all keys.

Preparatory Exercises to Nº 30.

Practise in all keys.

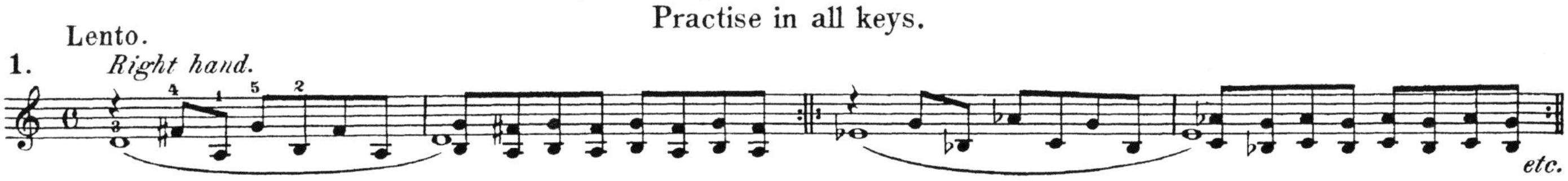

Preparatory Exercises to Nº 31.

Practise in all keys.

Vivace.

1. *Right hand.* Hold down all the fingers.

2. *Left hand.*

Vivace.

Hold down all the fingers.

31.

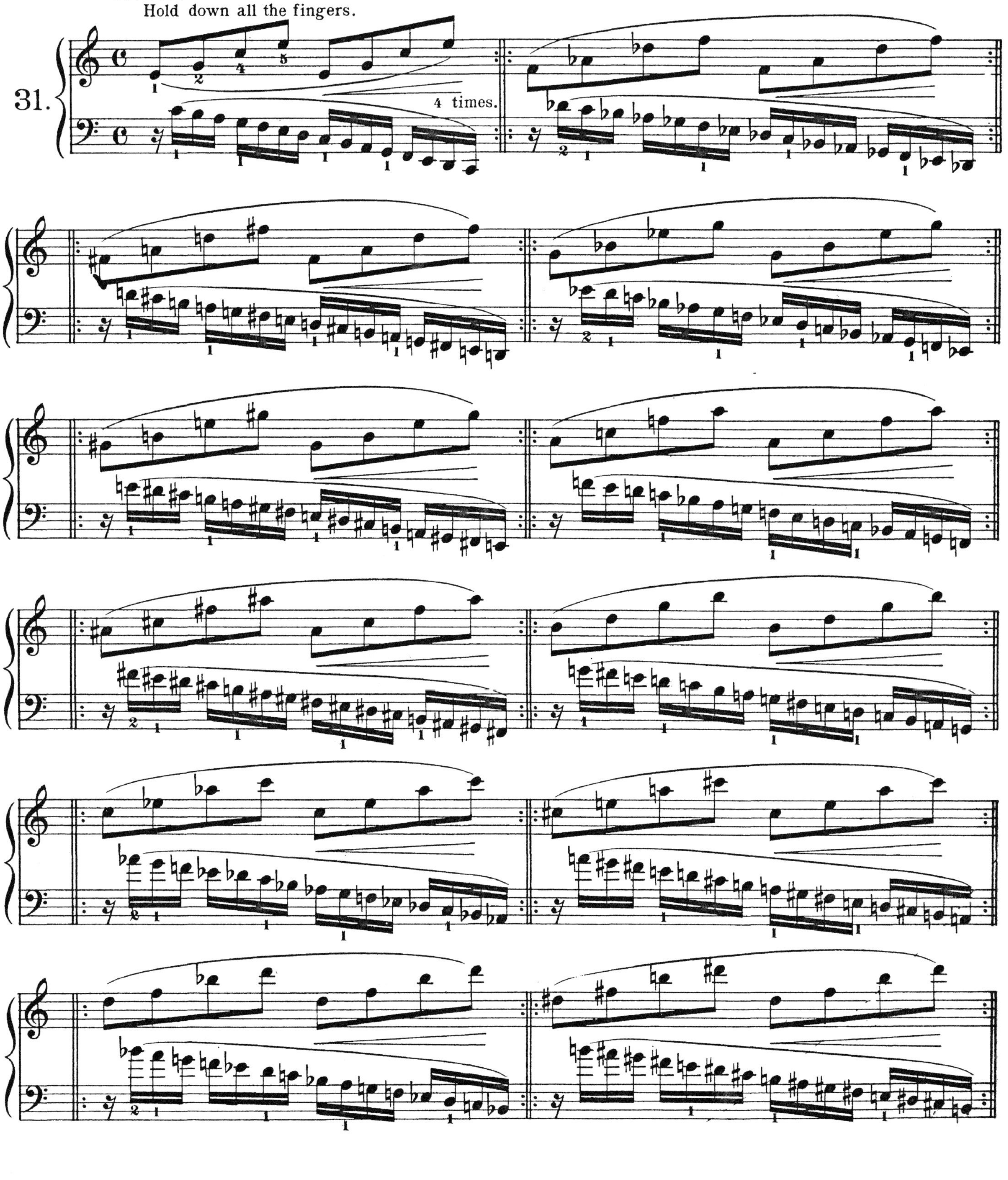

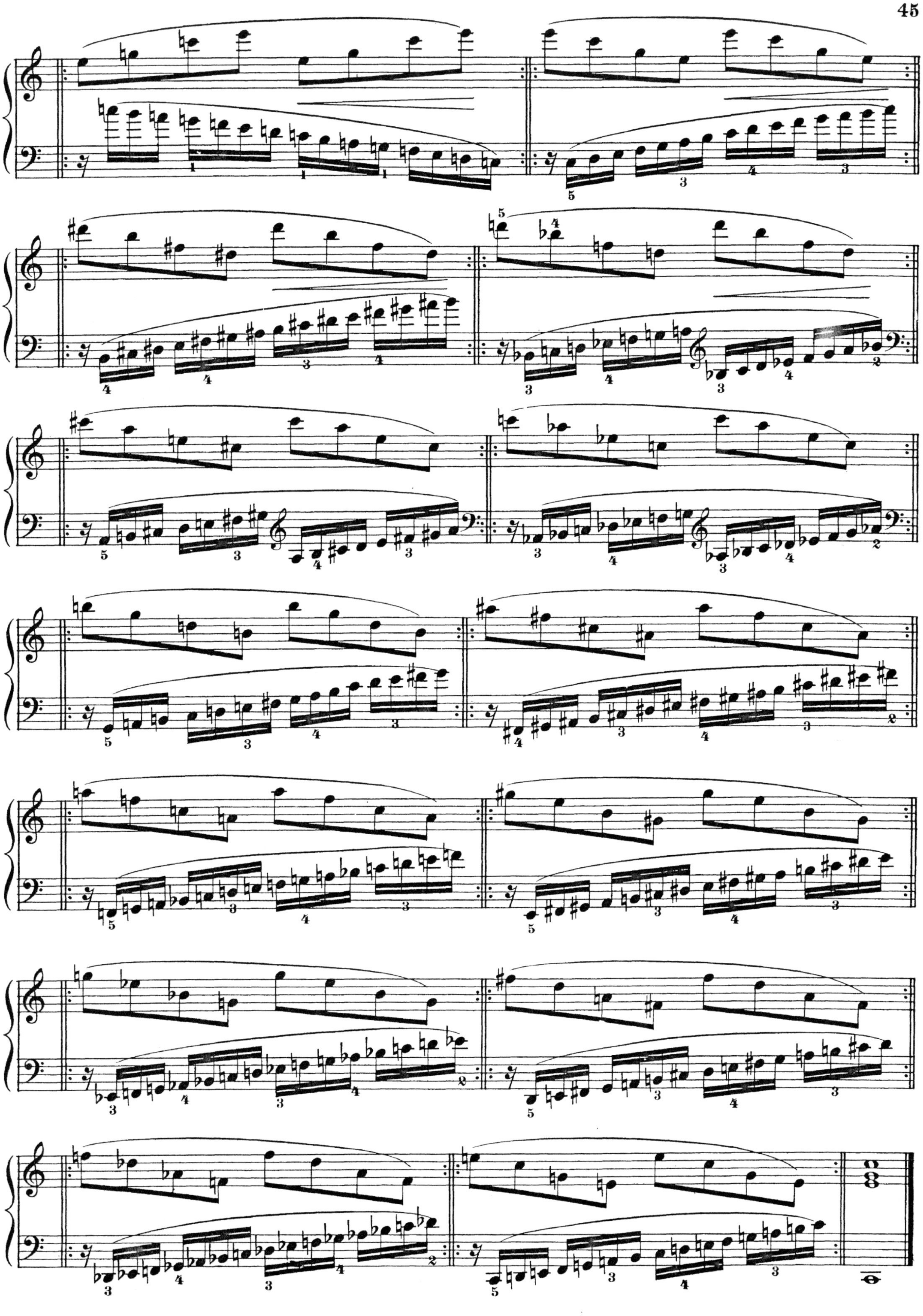

Preparatory Exercises to No. 32.

Practise in all keys.

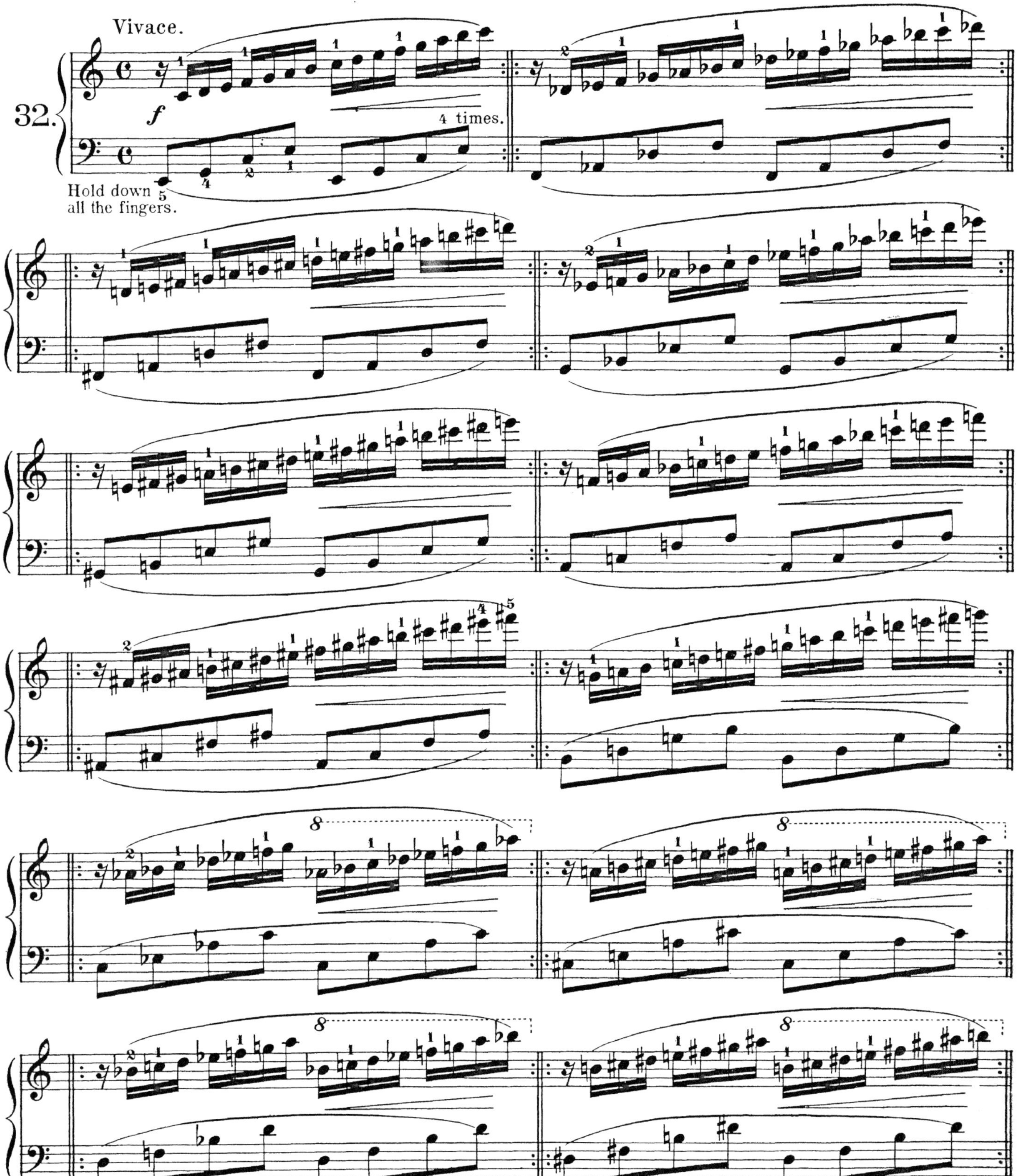

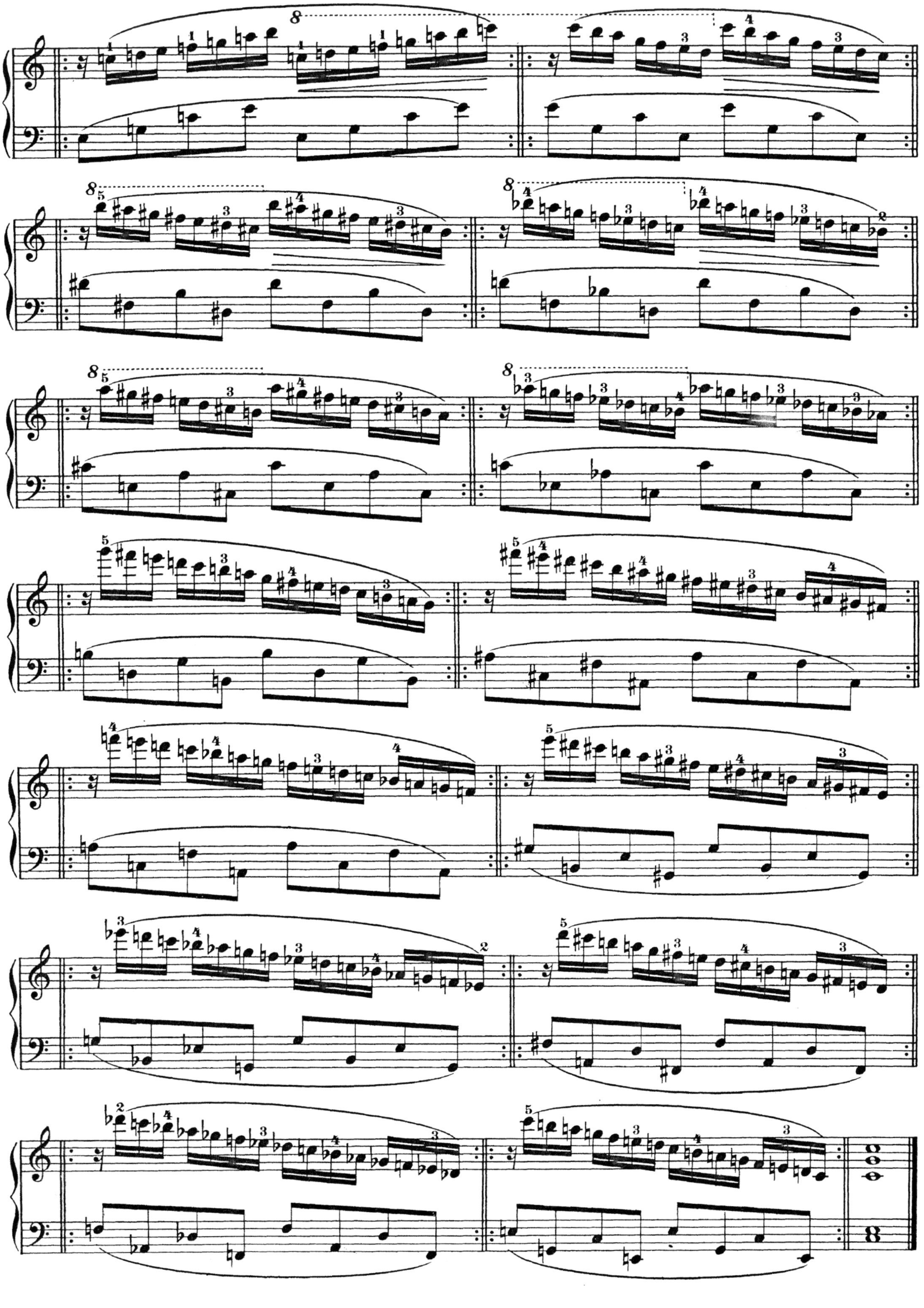

Moderato.

Hold down all the fingers.

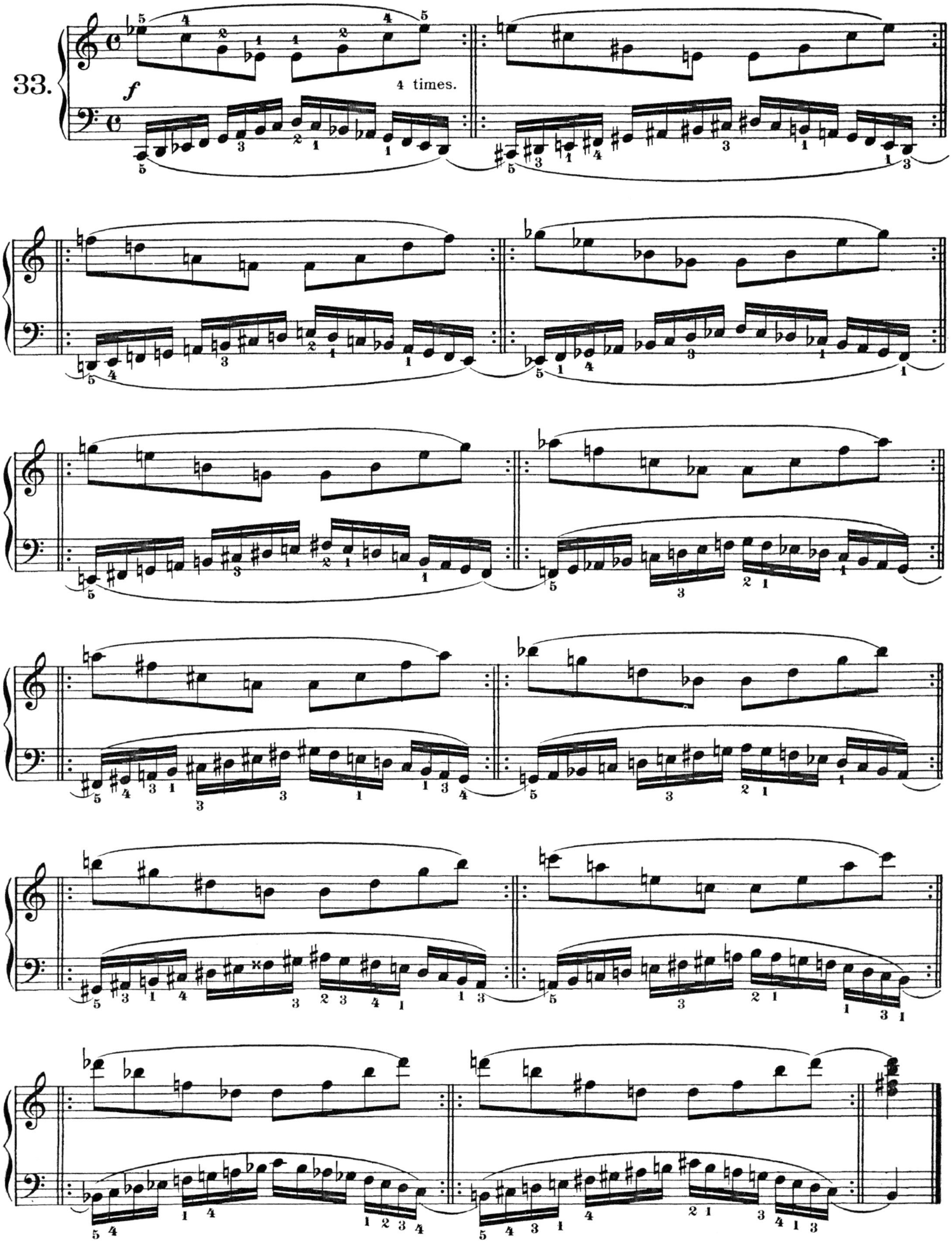

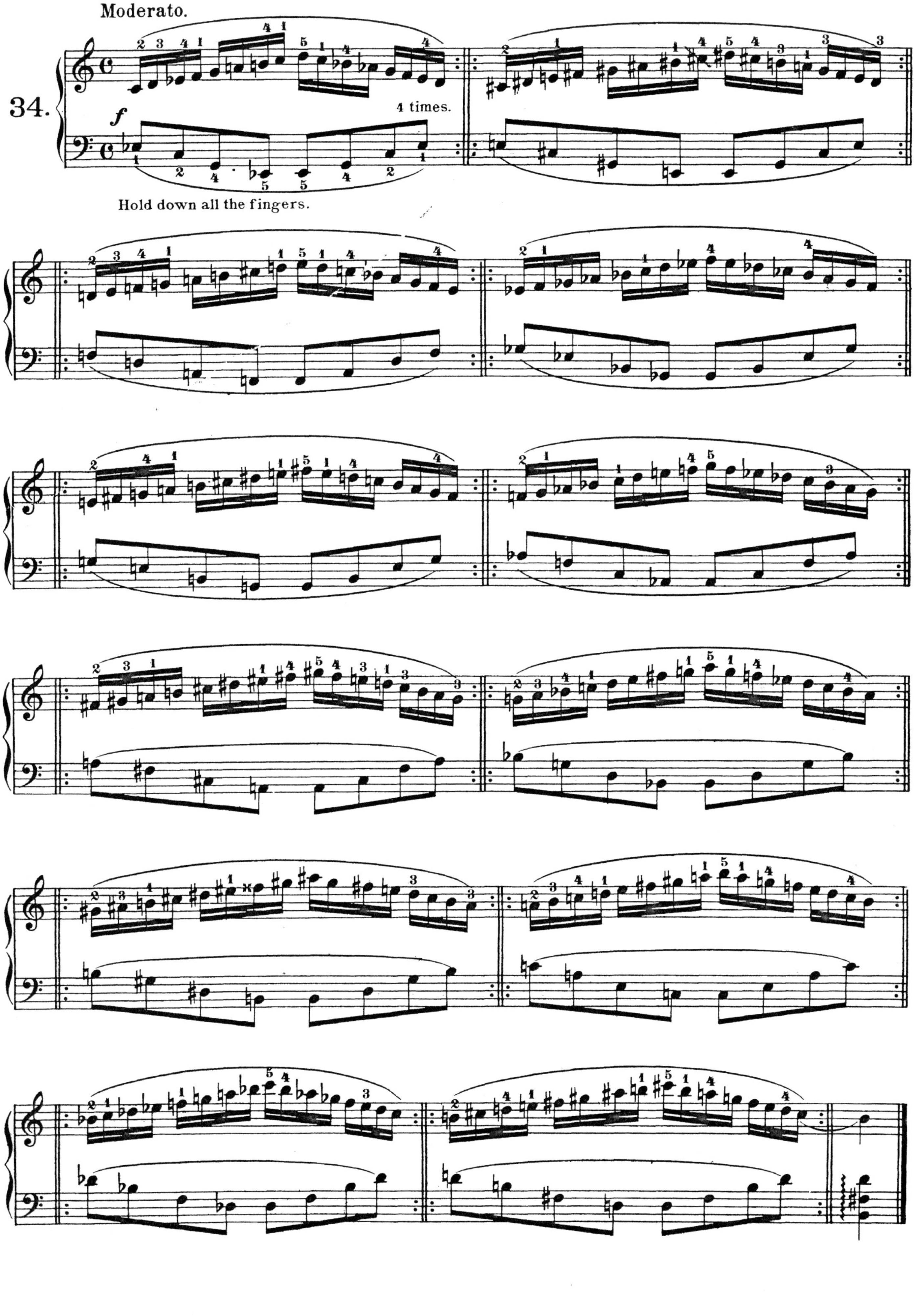
Moderato.
34.
4 times.
Hold down all the fingers.

Preparatory Exercises to No. 35.

Practise in all keys.

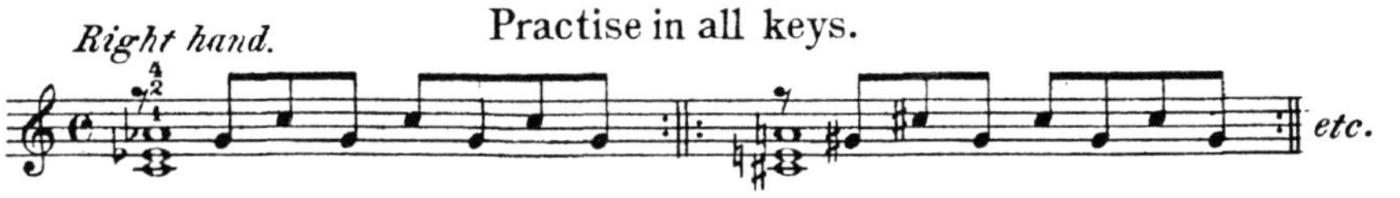

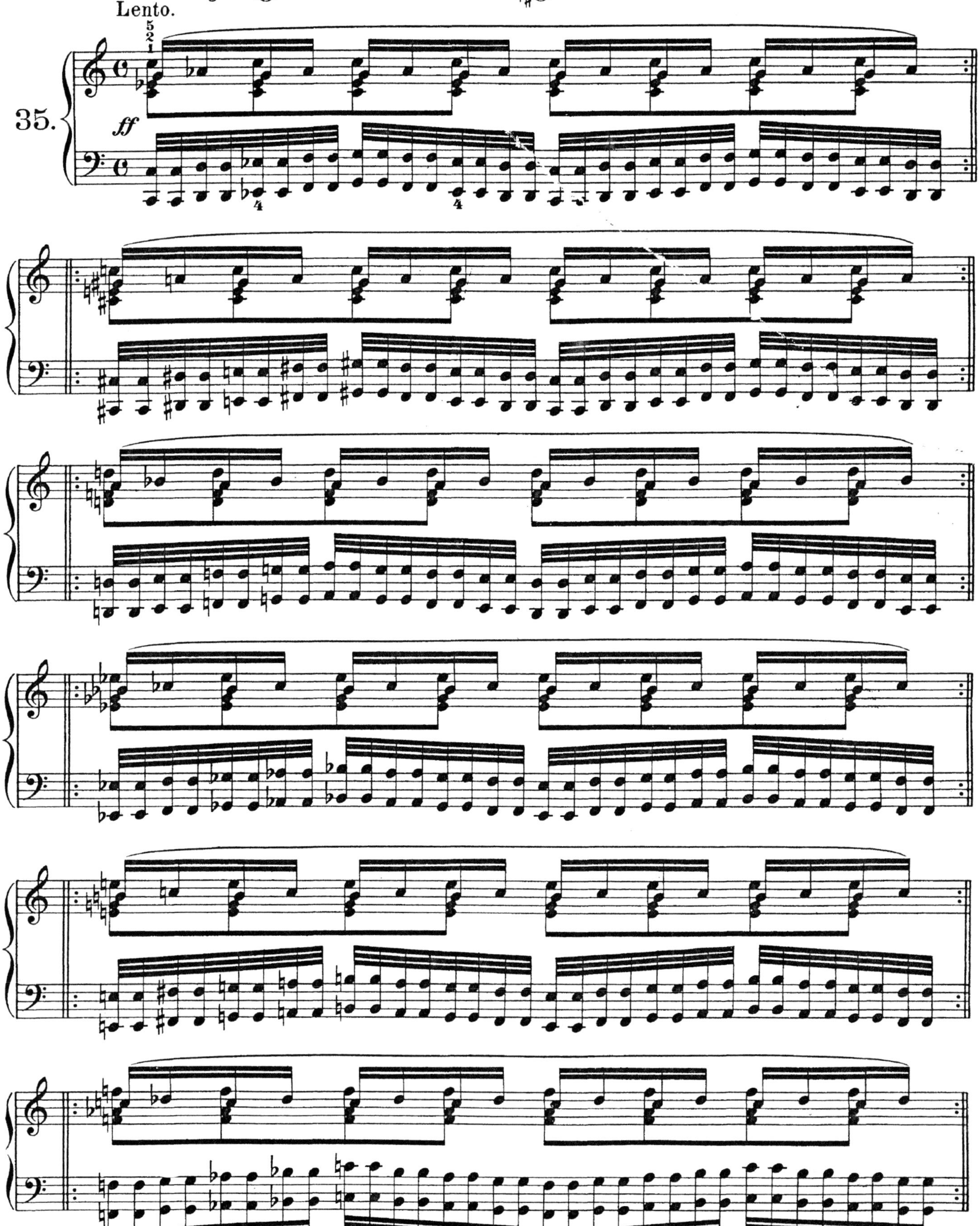

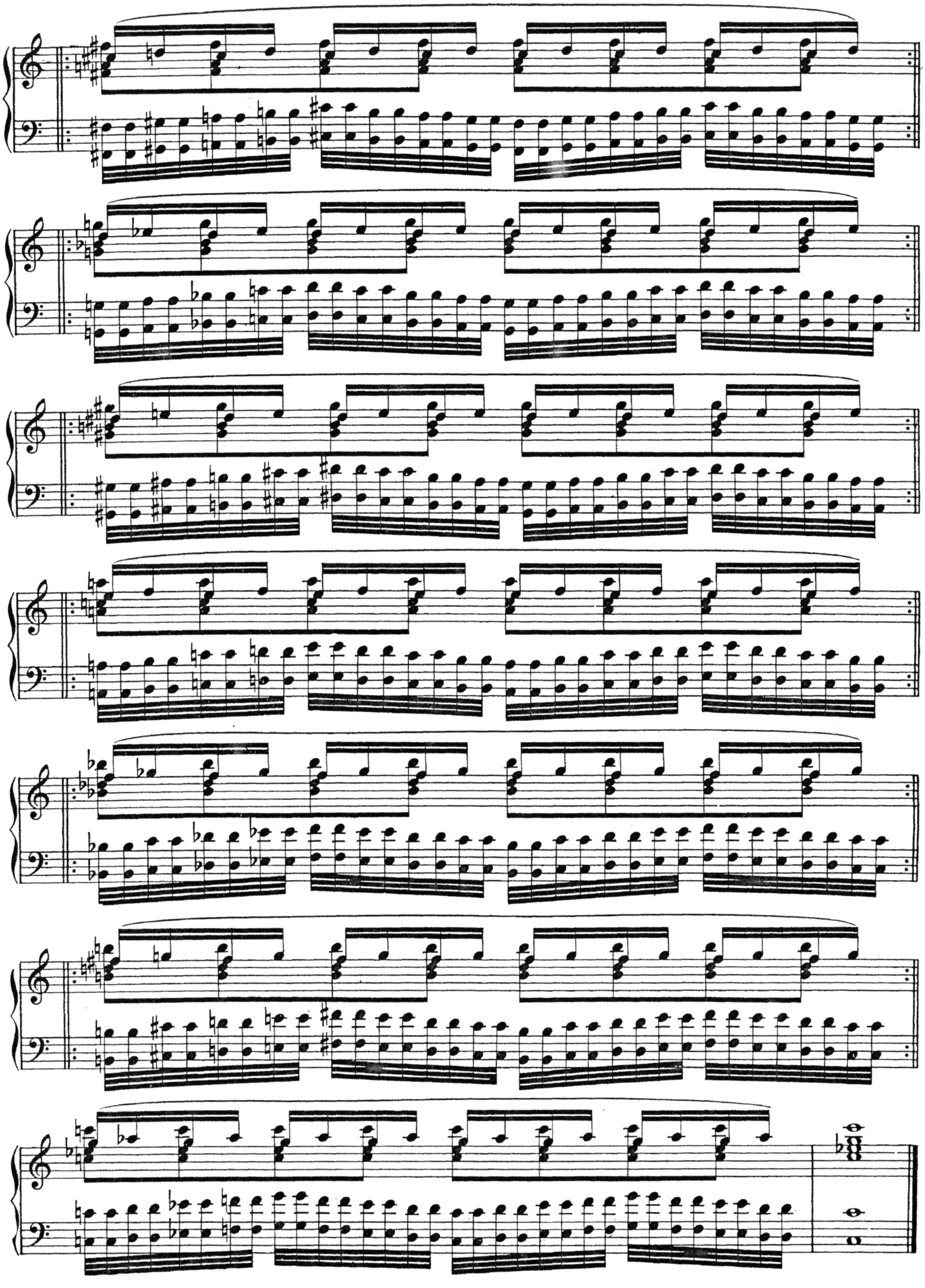

Preparatory Exercises to No. 36.

Practise in all keys.

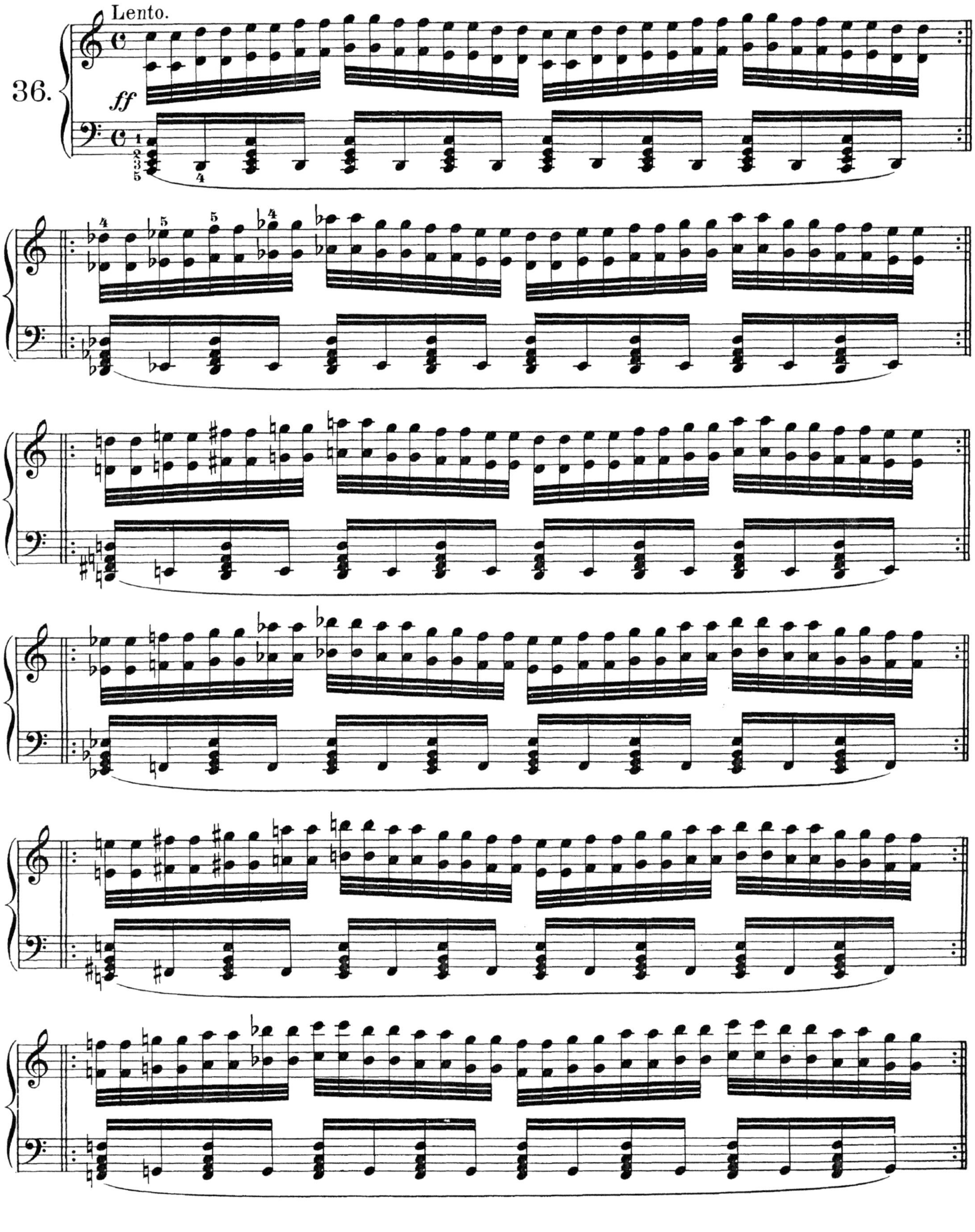

Preparatory Exercises to Nº 37.

Practise in all keys.

f
f

Preparatory Exercises to No. 38.

Practise in all keys.

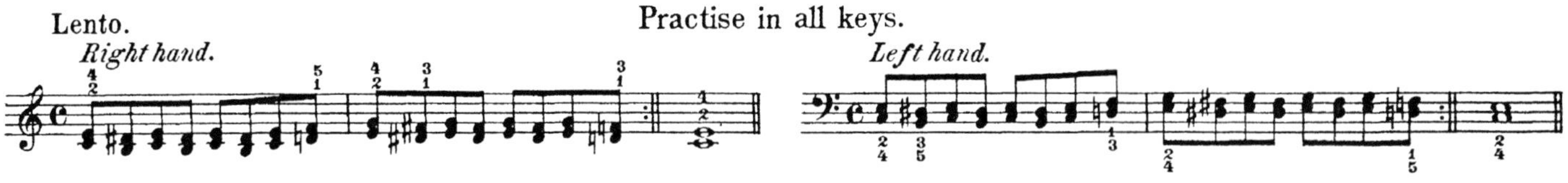

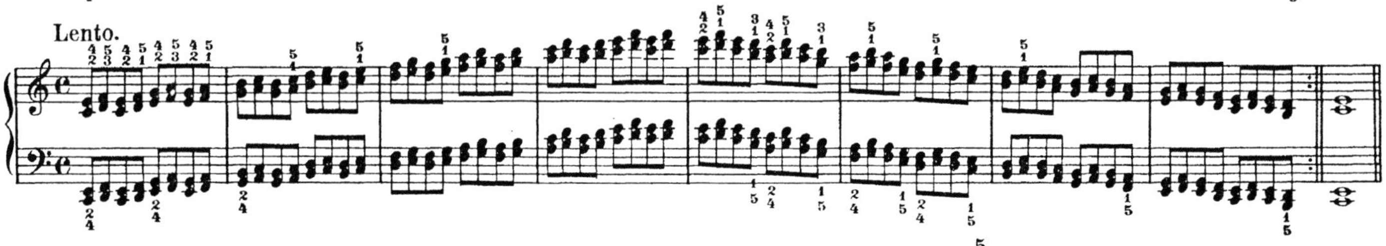

Preparatory Exercises to No. 39.

Practise in all keys.

*) With the same fingering in *G, D, A* and *E major*.

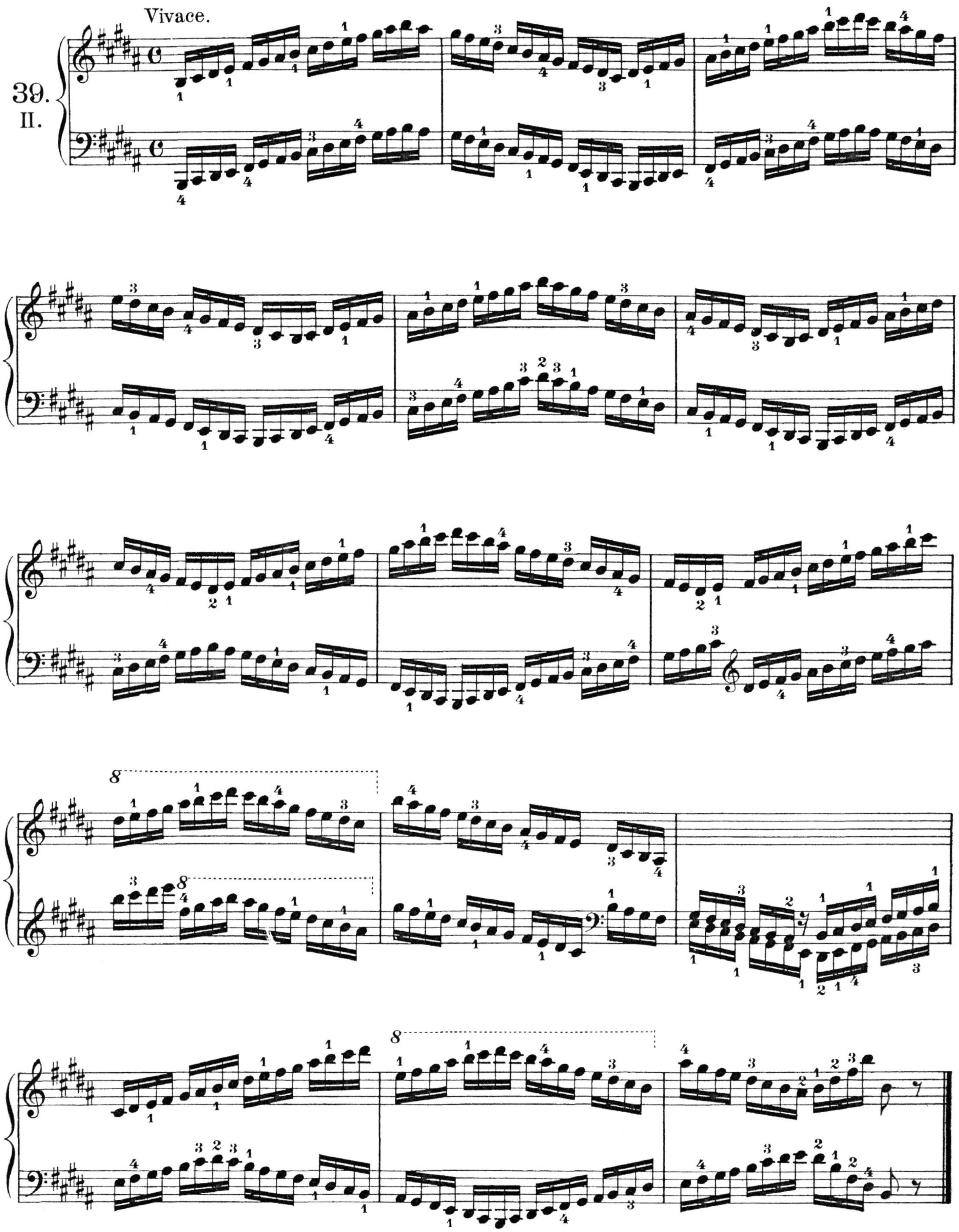
Vivace.
39.
II.

Vivace.
39.
III.

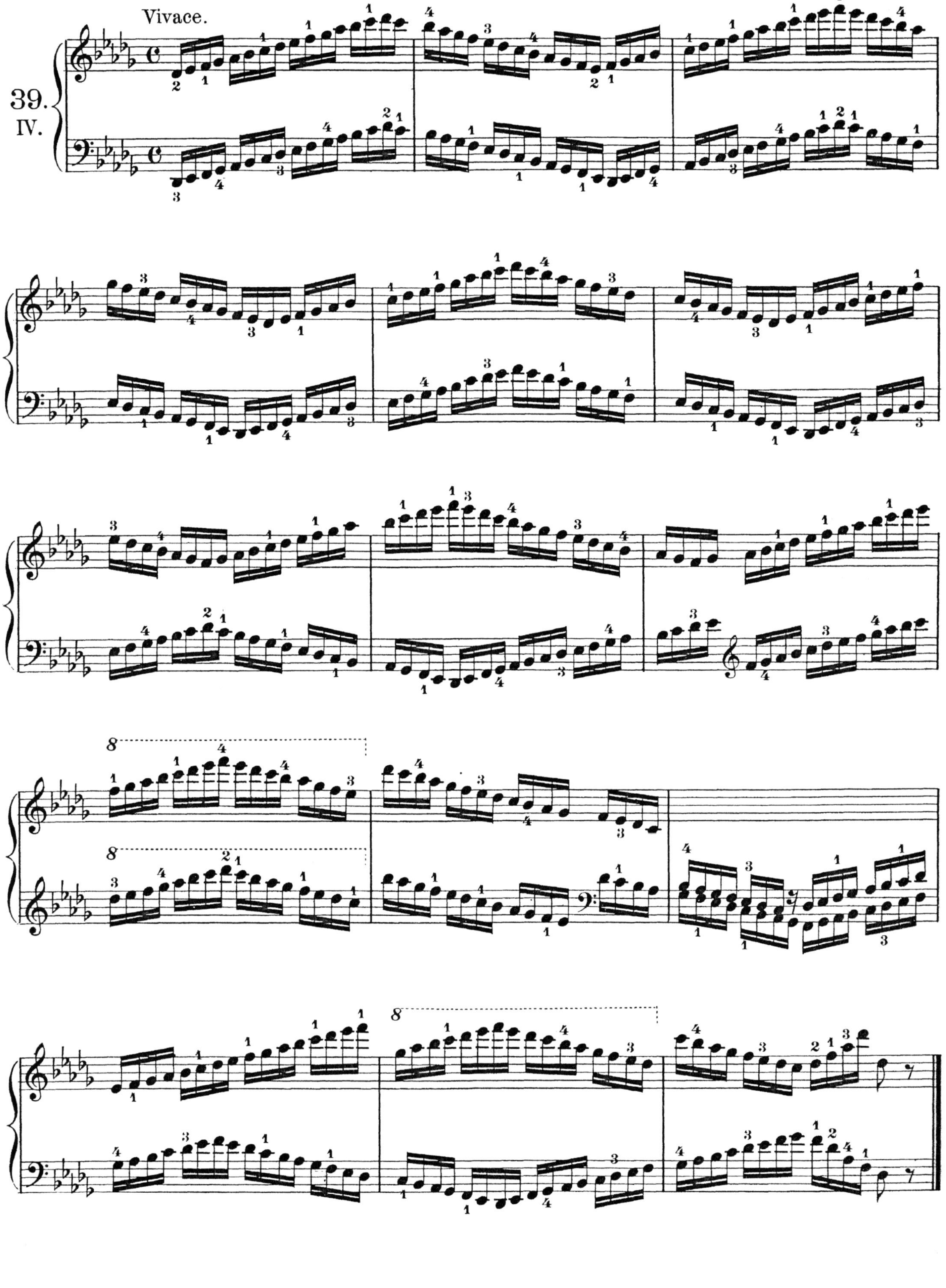
Vivace.
39.
IV.

Vivace.
39.
V.
8
8
8

Vivace.
39.
VI.

Vivace.
39.
VII.

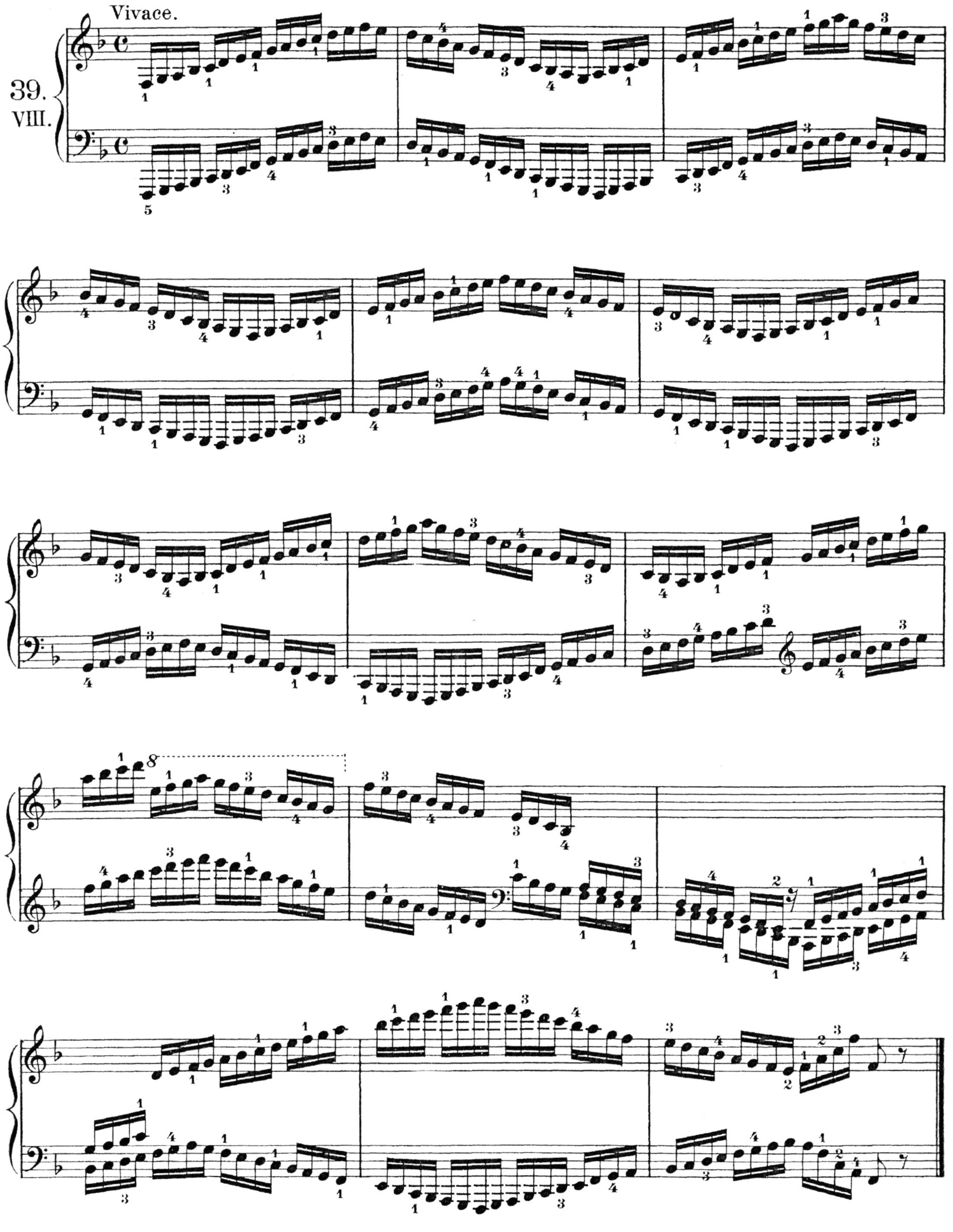
Vivace.
39.
VIII.

Preparatory Exercises to Nº 40.

Practise in all keys.

* With the same fingering in *E*, *C*, *G* and *D minor*.

Vivace.
40.
II.
8
8
8

Vivace.
40.
III.

Vivace.
40.
IV.

Vivace.
40.
V.

Vivace.
40.
VI.

Vivace.
40.
VII.

Vivace.
40.
VIII.

Preparatory Exercises to Nº 41.

Practise in all keys.

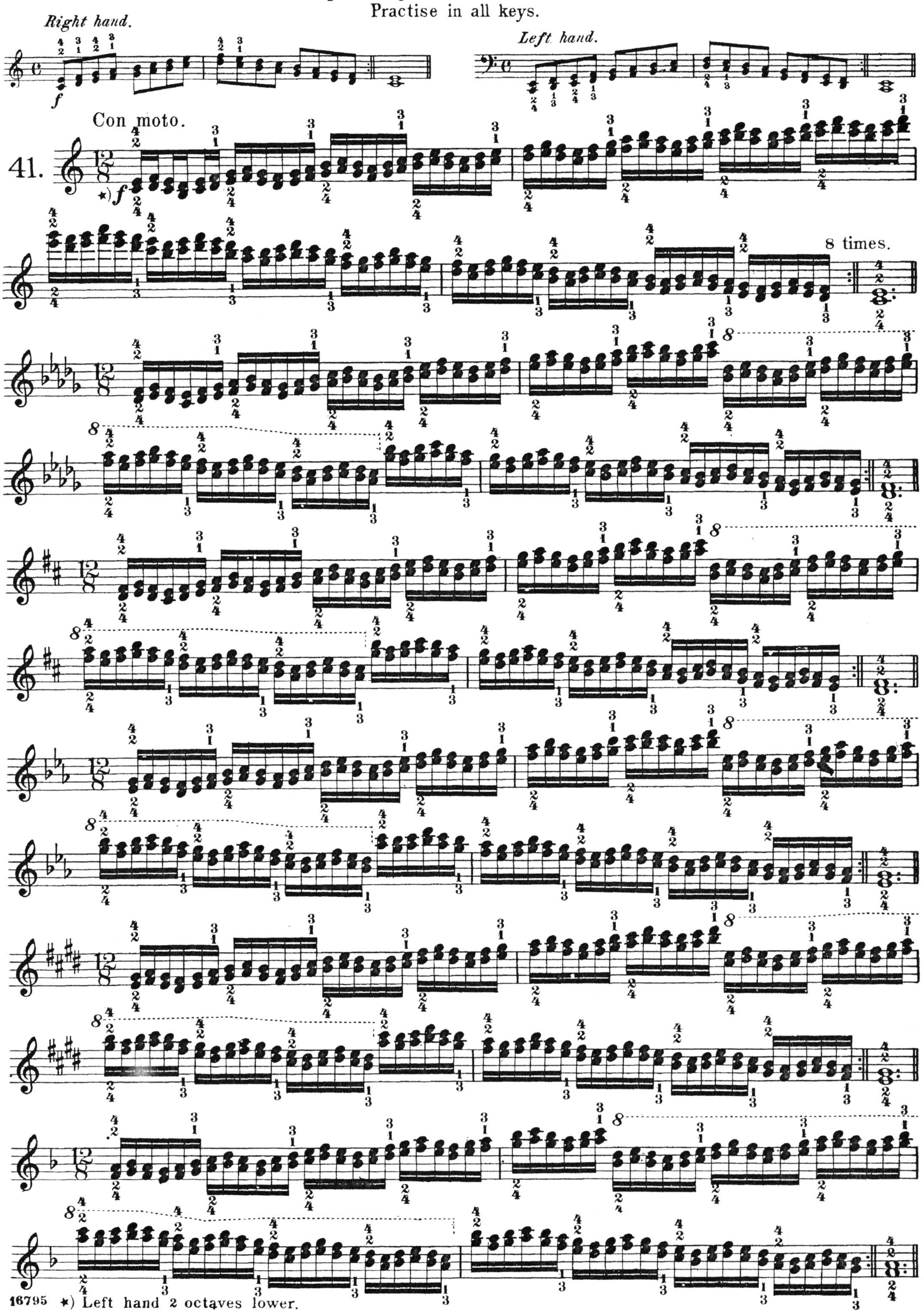

 *) Left hand 2 octaves lower.

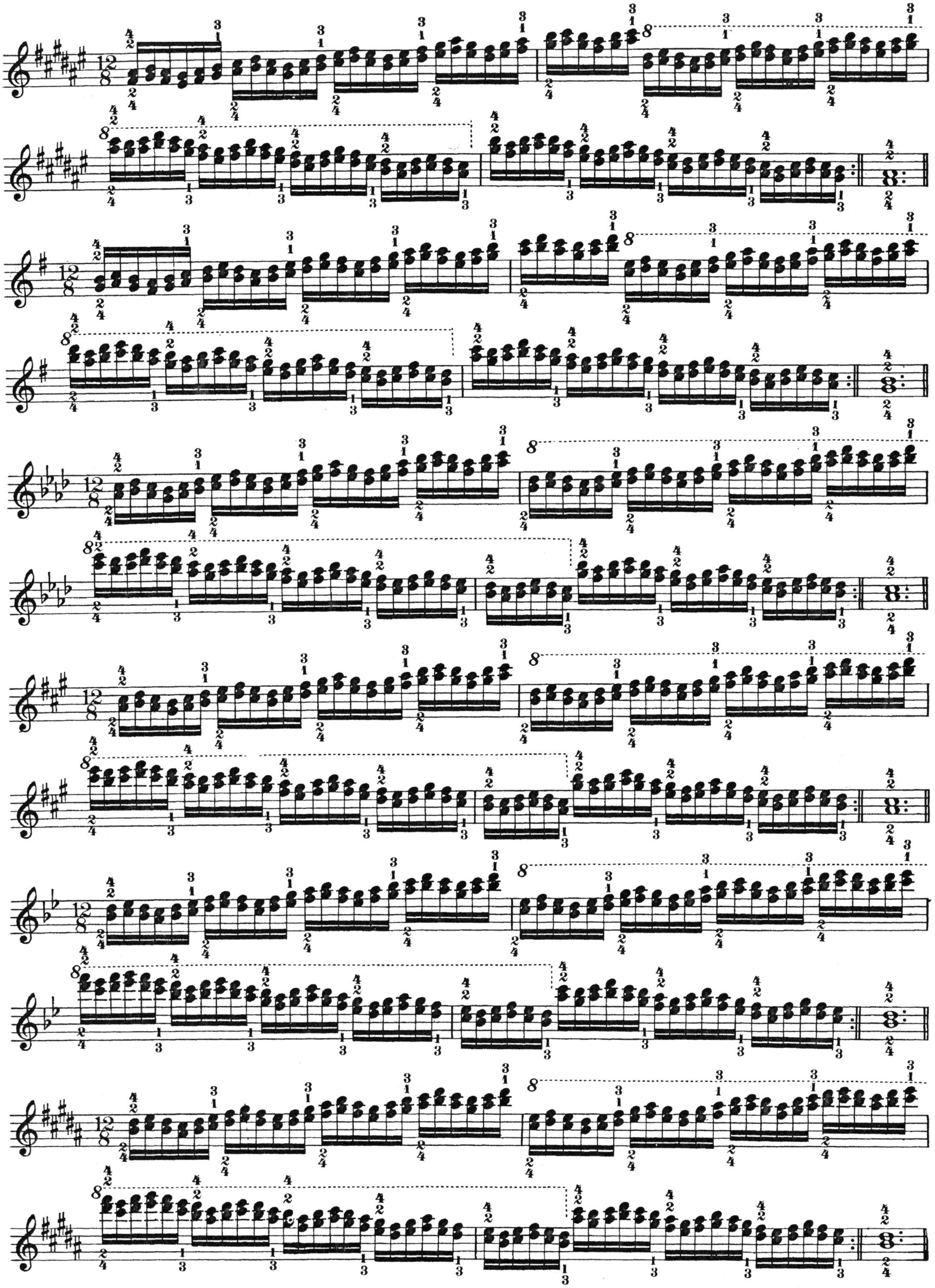

Preparatory Exercises to No. 42.

Practise in all keys.

Right hand.

Con moto.

Preparatory Exercises to Nº 43.

Practise in all keys.

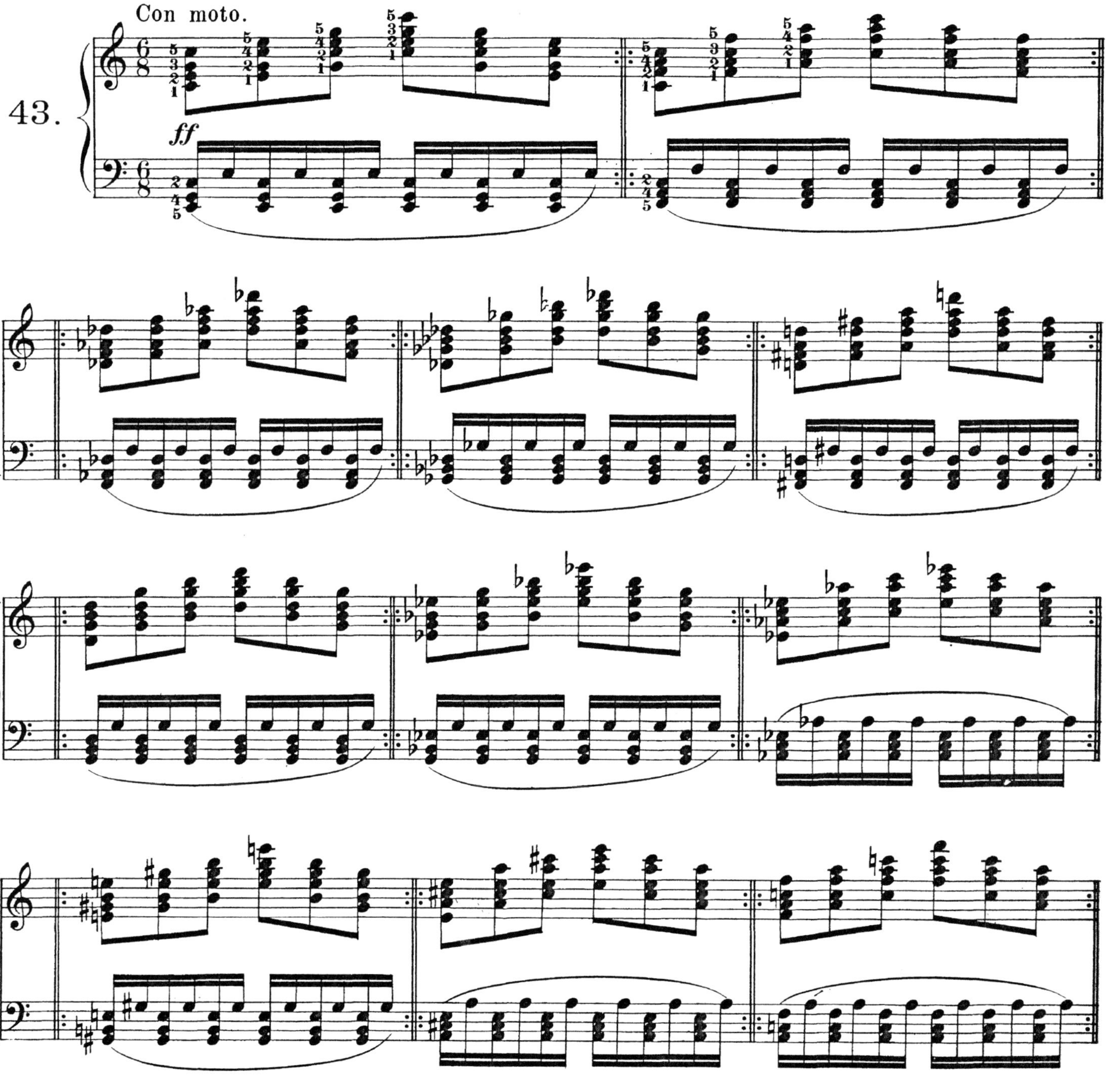

8
8

Preparatory Exercises to Nº 44.

Practise in all keys.

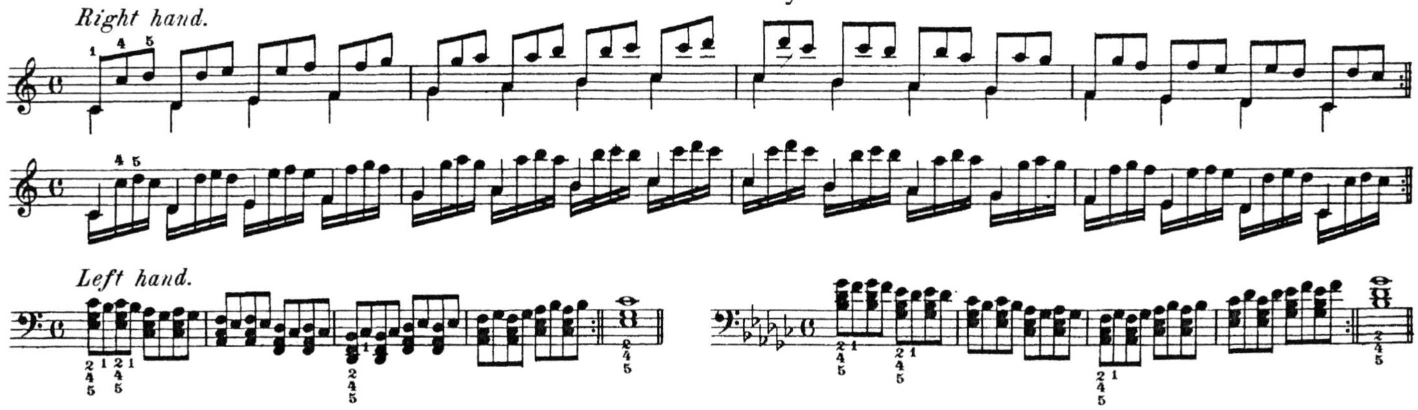

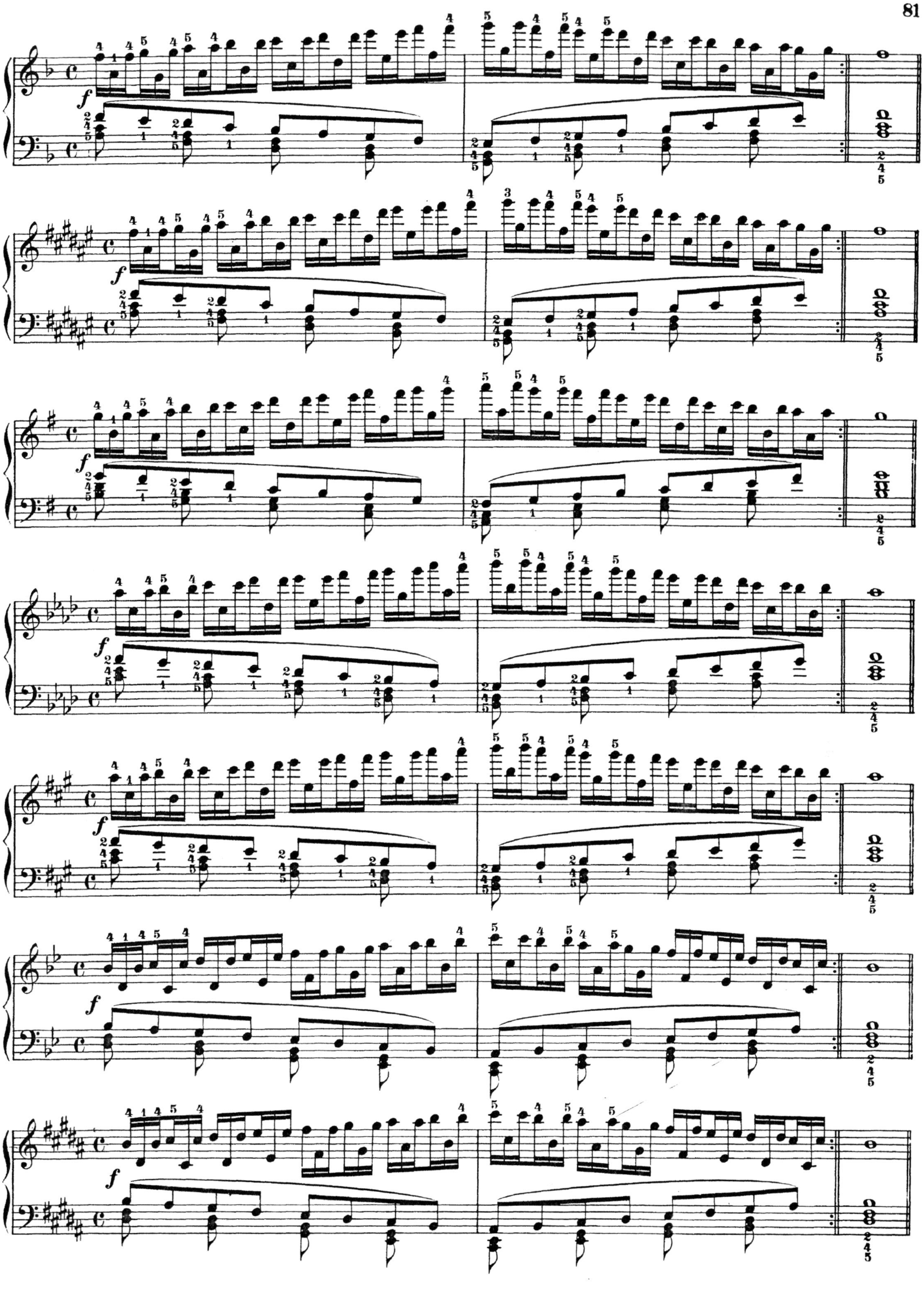

Preparatory Exercises to Nº 45.

Practise in all keys.

45.

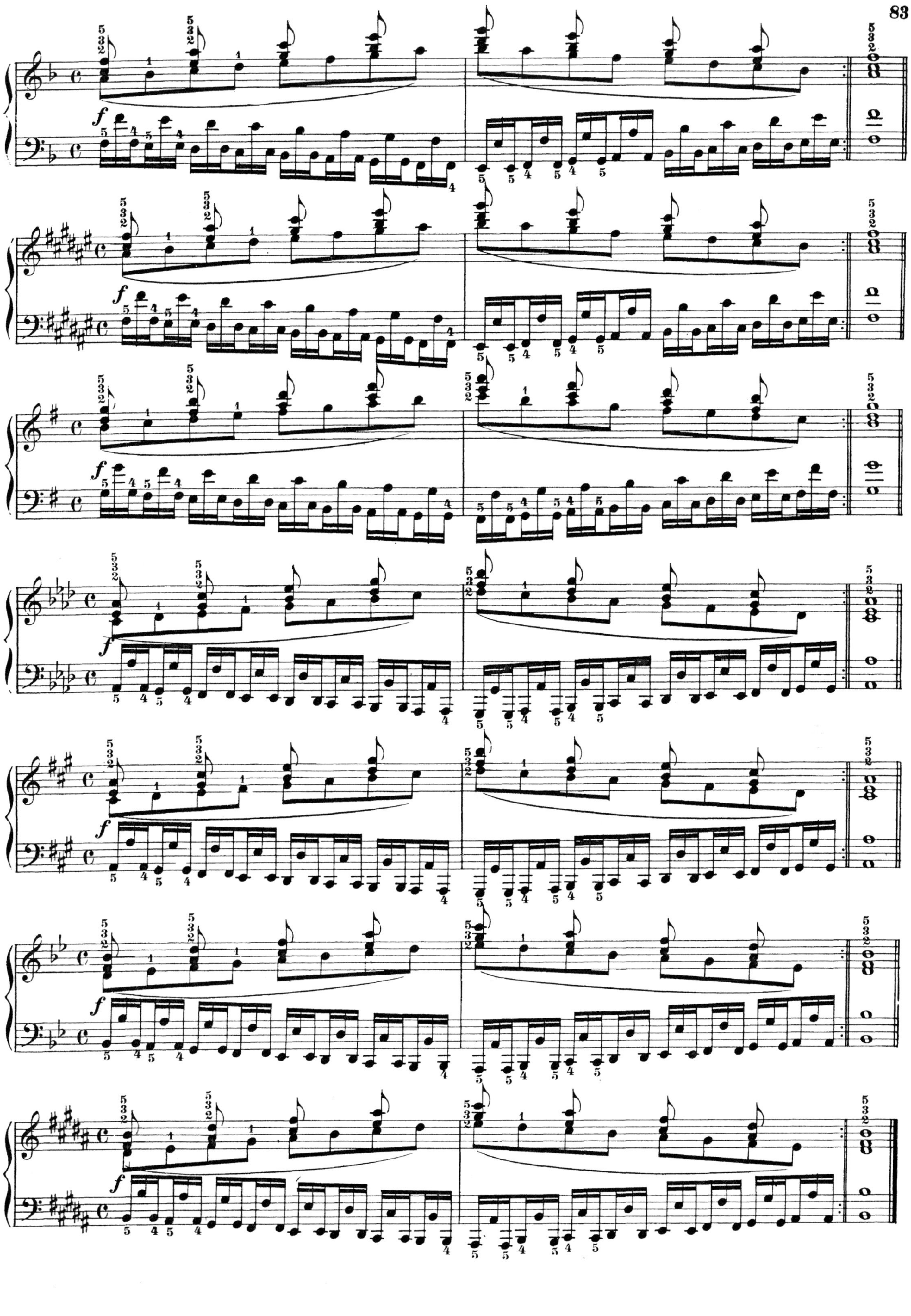

Preparatory Exercises to Nos 46 and 47.

Practise in all keys.

Left hand.
Hold down all the fingers.

Right hand.
Hold down all the fingers.

Hold down all the fingers.

Con moto.

46.

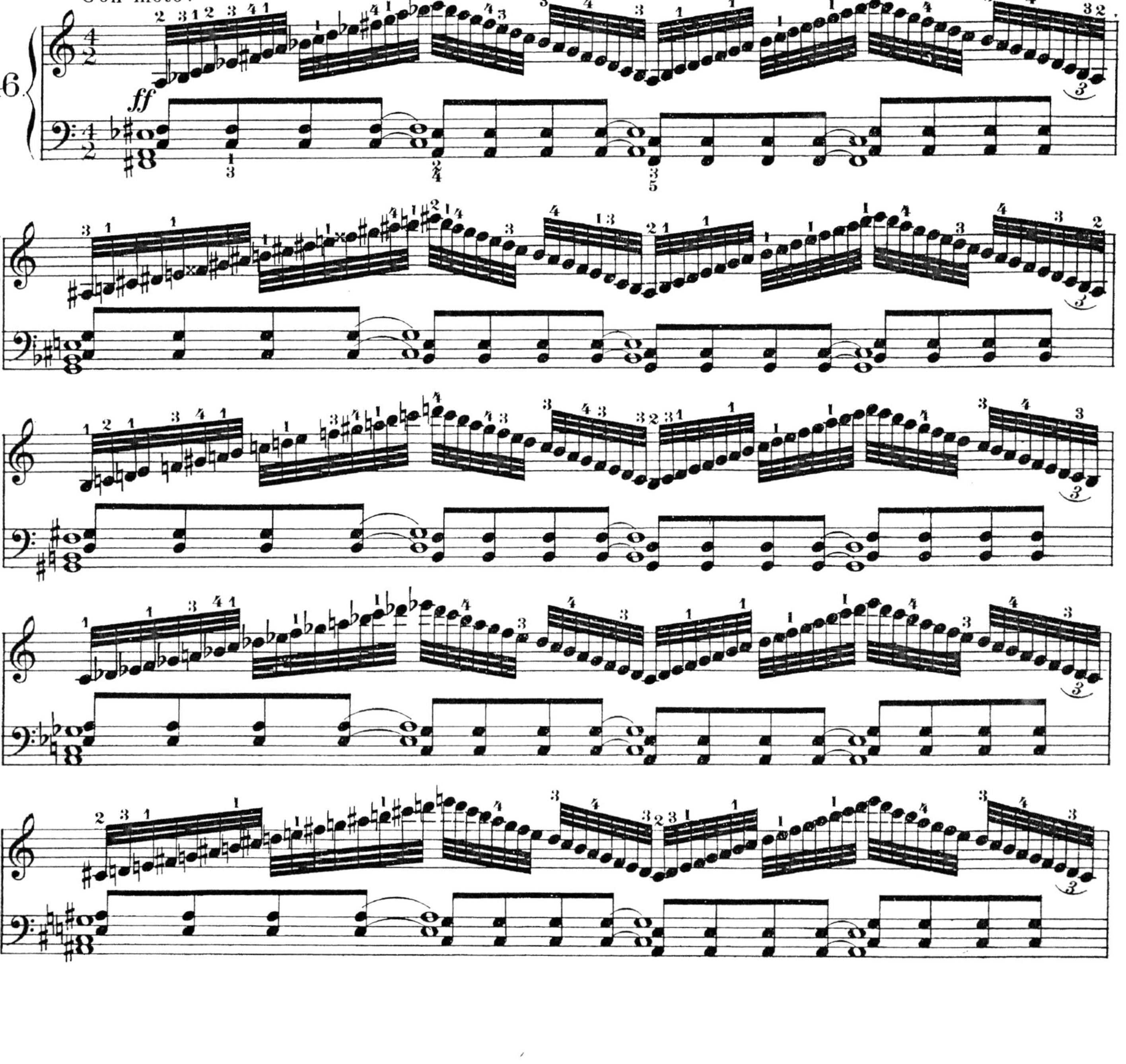

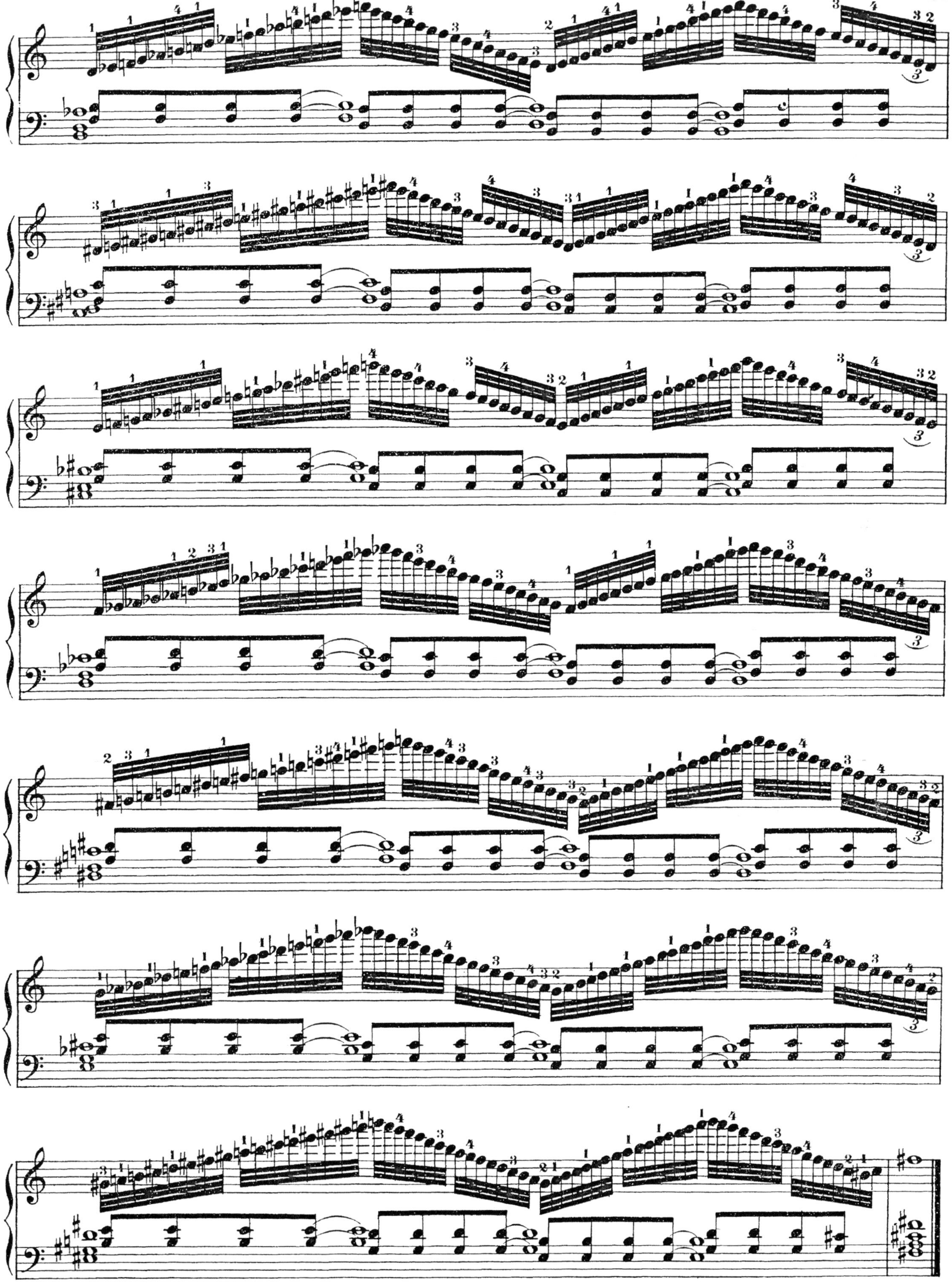

Con moto.

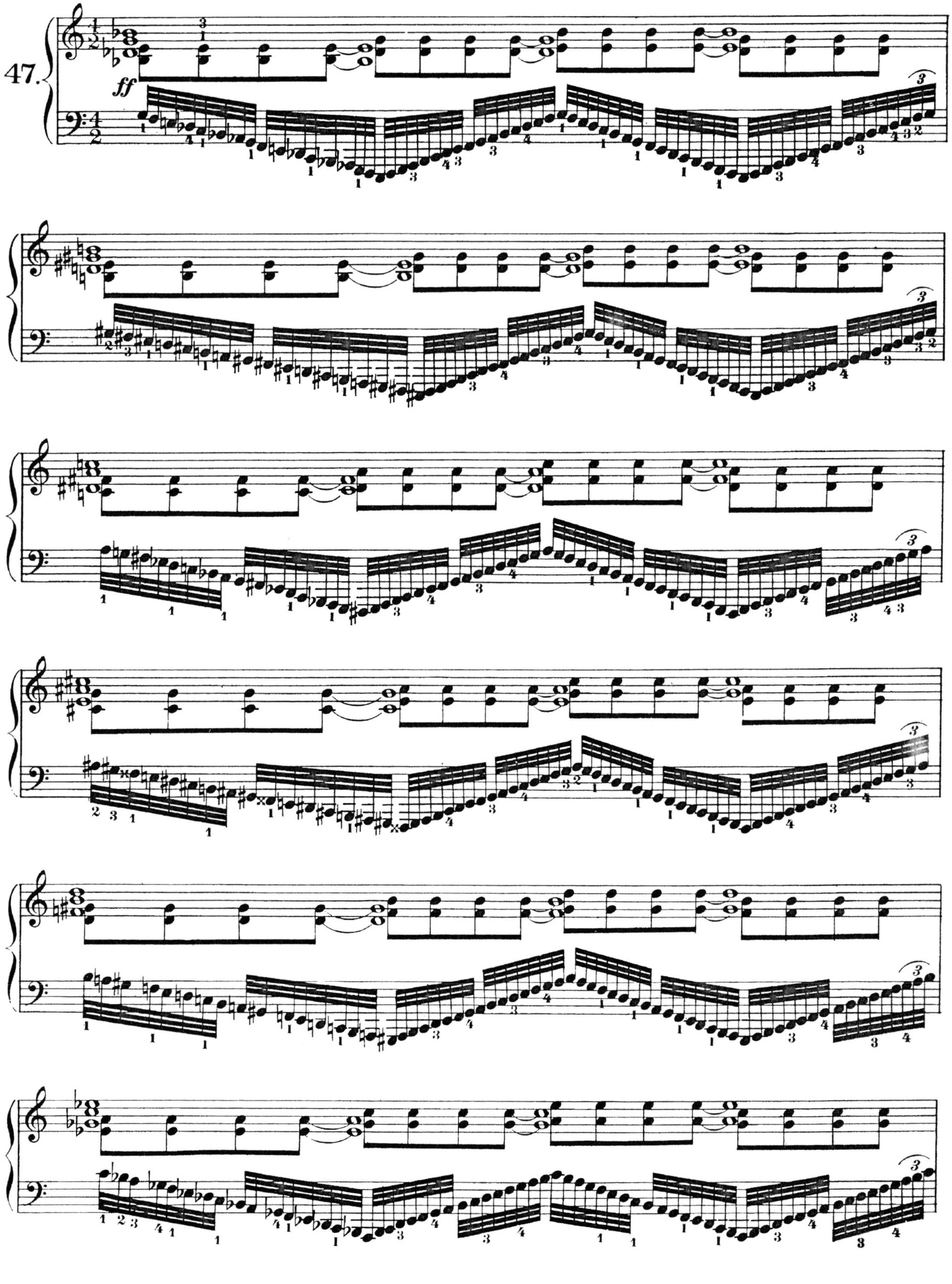

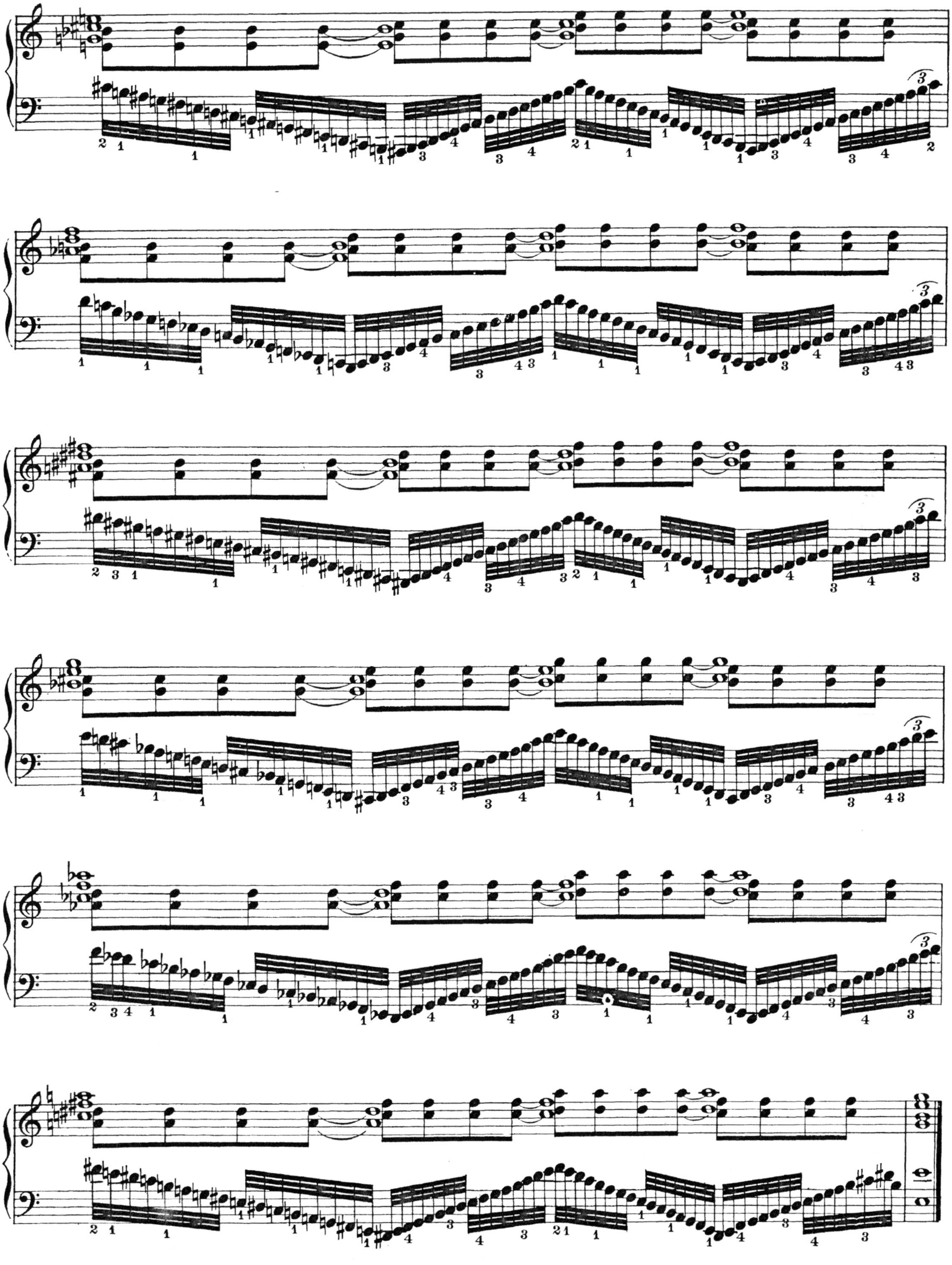

Veloce.
48.
f
8 times.

Allegro.
49.
f legato
8 times.

Allegro.
50.
f legato
8 times.

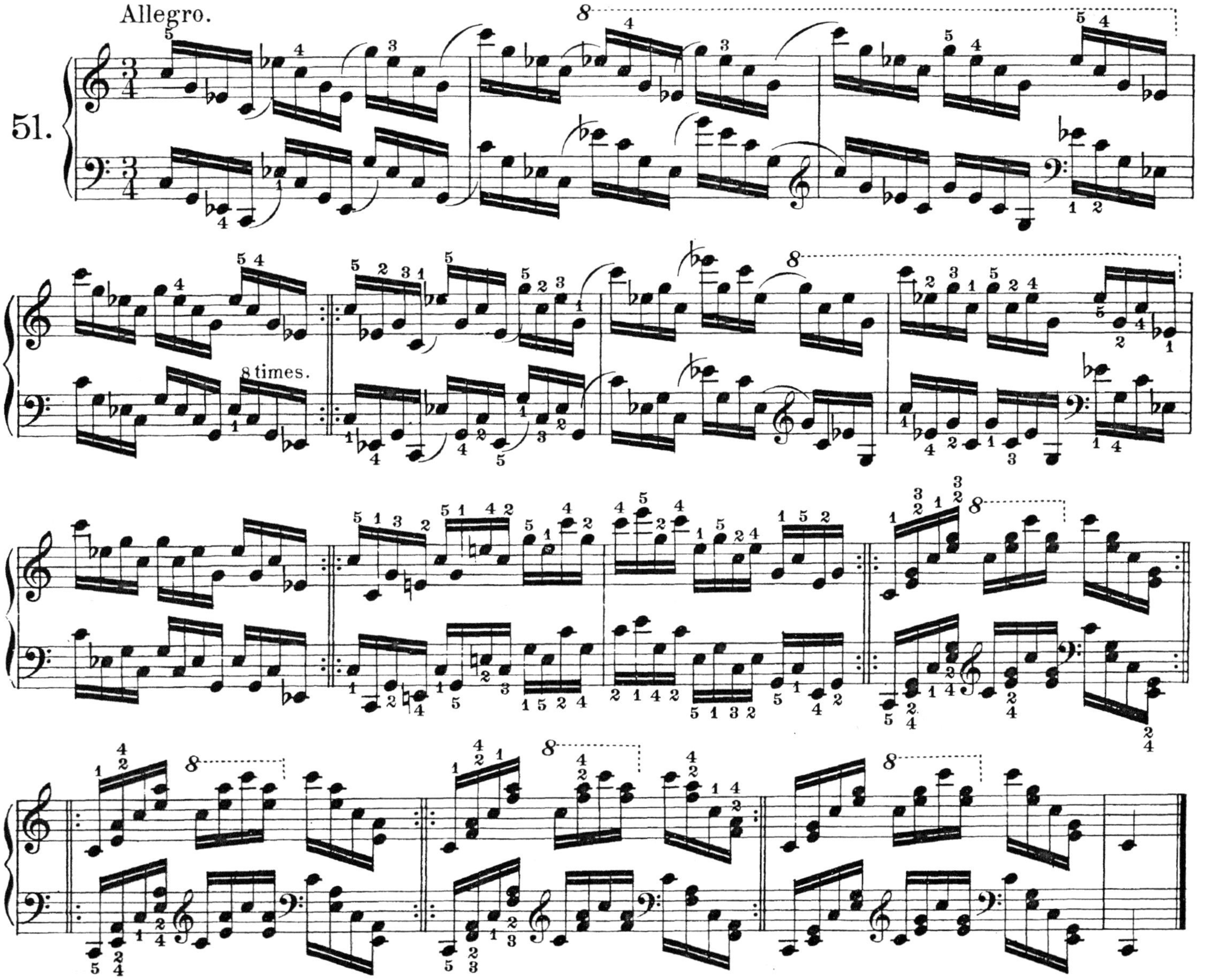
Allegro.
51.
8 times.

Lento.

52.

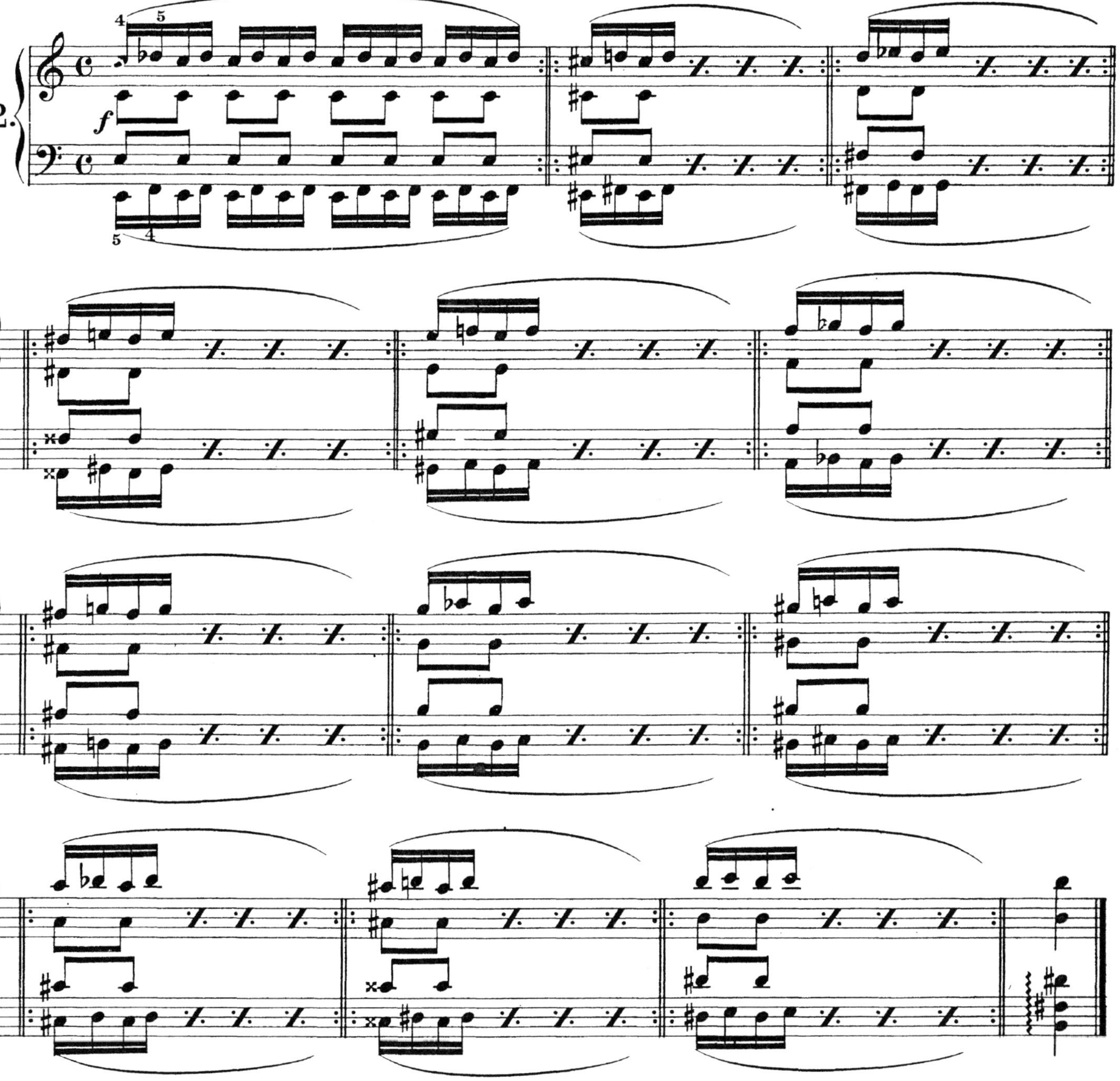

Preparatory Exercises to No. 53.

Practise in all keys.

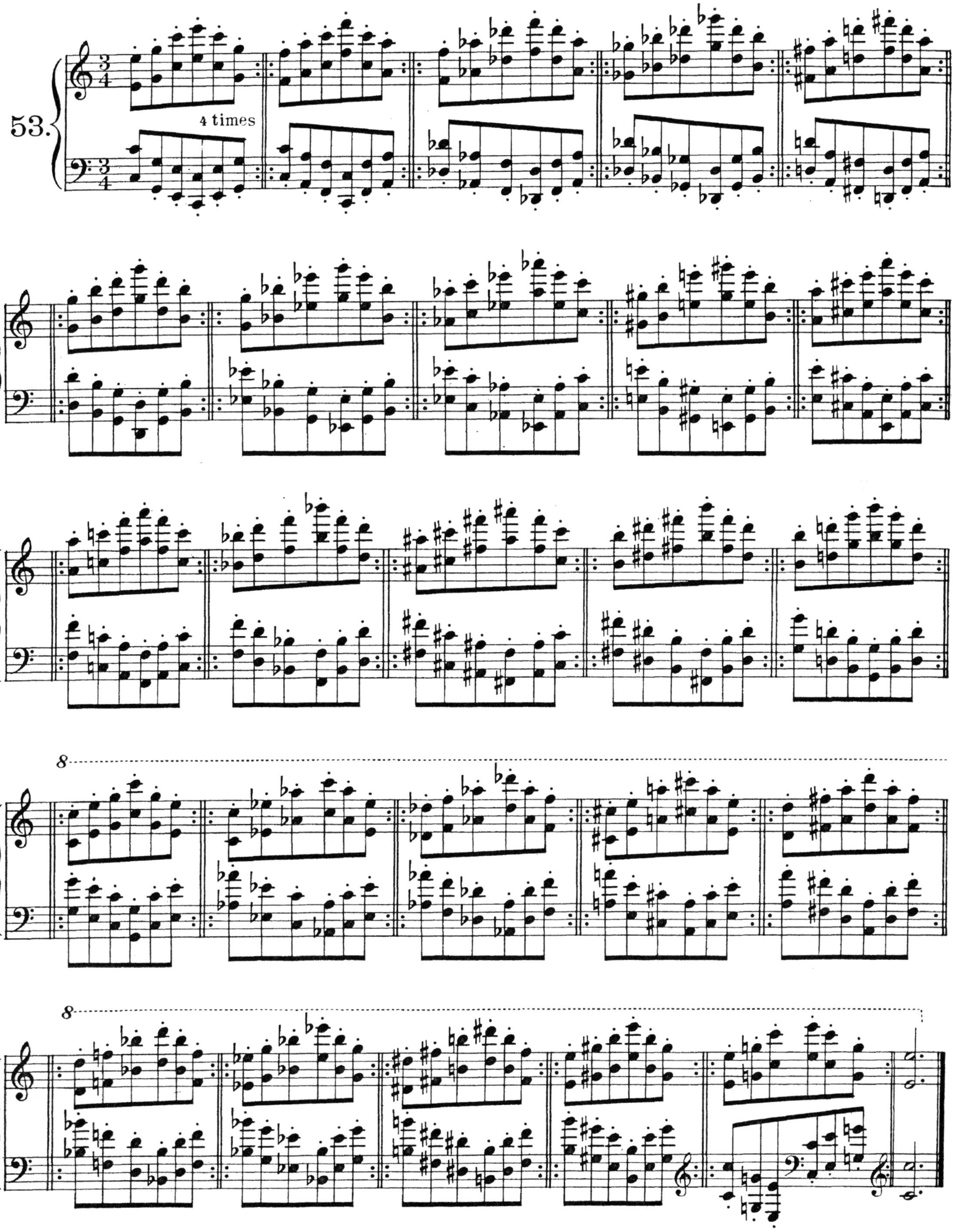
53.
4 times
8
8

Allegro.
54.
p
cresc.
f
decresc.

Allegro.
55.
p
cresc.
f
decresc.

Presto.
56.
8 times.

57.
ten.
Veloce.
58.

Preparatory Exercises to Nº 60.

H. Riemann.

Scales in Thirds.

Fingering acc. to Liszt-Tausig*)

H. Riemann.

*) The fingering of Chopin (Étude Op. 25, № 6, in G# minor) does not lead to the highest degree of precision:

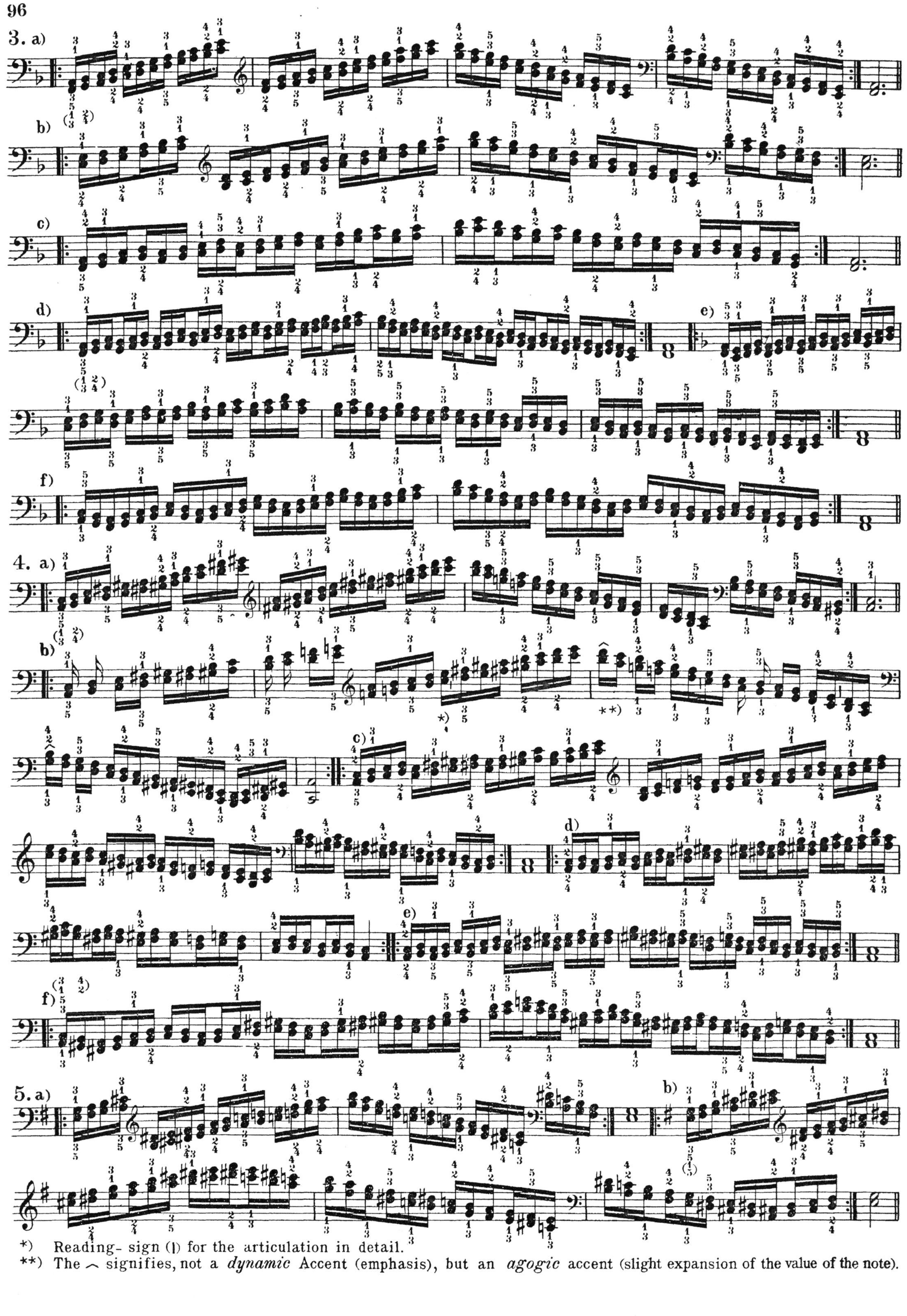

*) Reading- sign (|) for the articulation in detail.

**) The ⌢ signifies, not a *dynamic* Accent (emphasis), but an *agogic* accent (slight expansion of the value of the note).

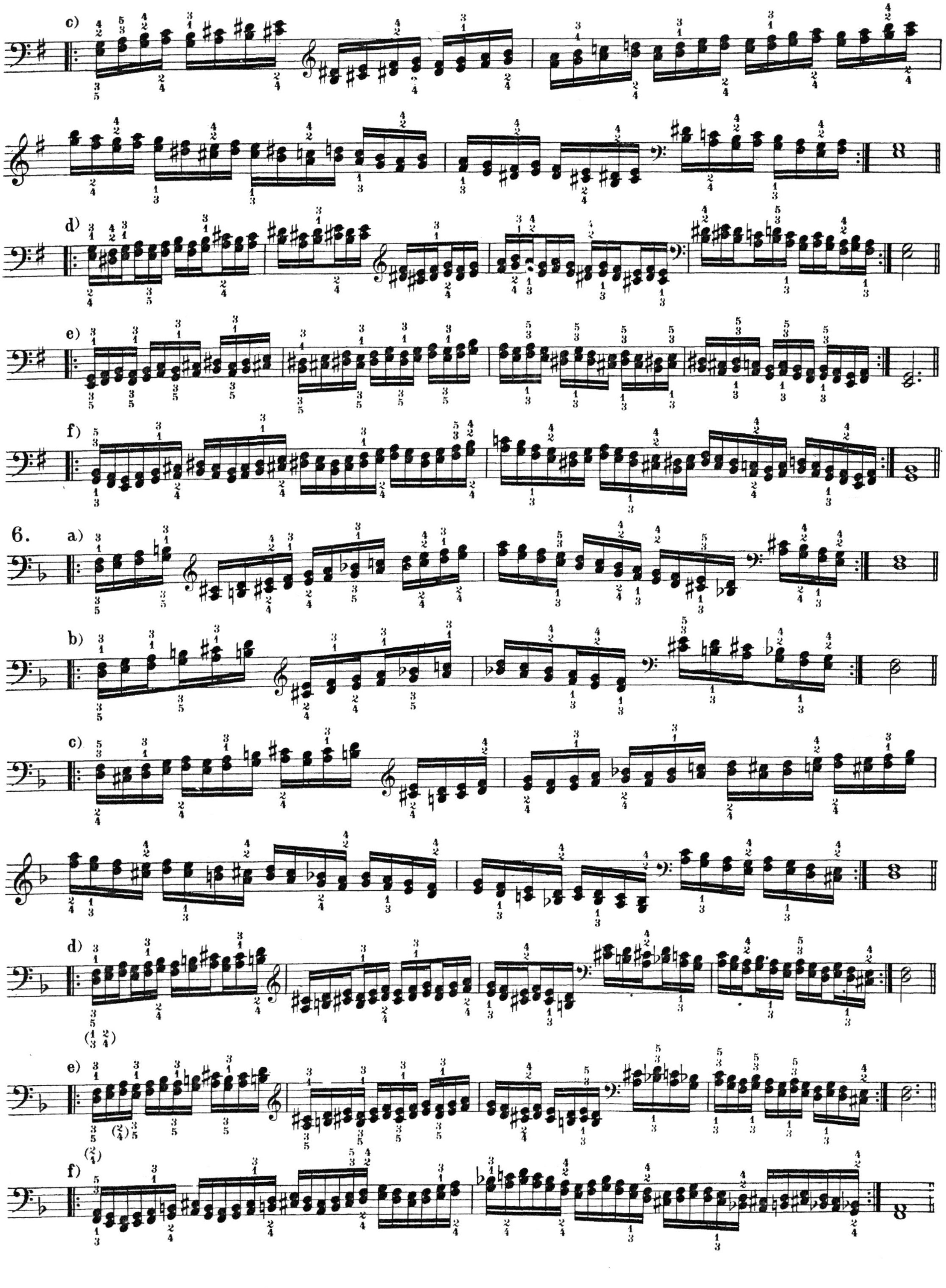
c)
d)
e)
f)
6.
a)
b)
c)
d)
e)
f)

7.
ossia
8.
ossia
9.
ossia
10.
ossia
11.
ossia
12.
ossia
13.
ossia
14.
ossia
15.
ossia
16.
ossia

17.
ossia
18.
ossia
19.
ossia
20.
ossia
21.
ossia
22.
ossia
23.
ossia
24.
ossia
25. (chromatic)